C-2344 CAREER EXAMINATION SERIES

This is your PASSBOOK for...

Personnel Analyst

Test Preparation Study Guide Questions & Answers

NATIONAL LEARNING CORPORATION®

National Learning Corporation

212 Michael Drive, Syosset, NY 11791
(516) 921-8888 • www.passbooks.com
E-mail: info@passbooks.com

PUBLISHED IN THE UNITED STATES OF AMERICA

PASSBOOK® SERIES

THE *PASSBOOK® SERIES* has been created to prepare applicants and candidates for the ultimate academic battlefield – the examination room.

At some time in our lives, each and every one of us may be required to take an examination – for validation, matriculation, admission, qualification, registration, certification, or licensure.

Based on the assumption that every applicant or candidate has met the basic formal educational standards, has taken the required number of courses, and read the necessary texts, the *PASSBOOK® SERIES* furnishes the one special preparation which may assure passing with confidence, instead of failing with insecurity. Examination questions – together with answers – are furnished as the basic vehicle for study so that the mysteries of the examination and its compounding difficulties may be eliminated or diminished by a sure method.

This book is meant to help you pass your examination provided that you qualify and are serious in your objective.

The entire field is reviewed through the huge store of content information which is succinctly presented through a provocative and challenging approach – the question-and-answer method.

A climate of success is established by furnishing the correct answers at the end of each test.

You soon learn to recognize types of questions, forms of questions, and patterns of questioning. You may even begin to anticipate expected outcomes.

You perceive that many questions are repeated or adapted so that you can gain acute insights, which may enable you to score many sure points.

You learn how to confront new questions, or types of questions, and to attack them confidently and work out the correct answers.

You note objectives and emphases, and recognize pitfalls and dangers, so that you may make positive educational adjustments.

Moreover, you are kept fully informed in relation to new concepts, methods, practices, and directions in the field.

You discover that you are actually taking the examination all the time: you are preparing for the examination by "taking" an examination, not by reading extraneous and/or supererogatory textbooks.

In short, this PASSBOOK®, used directedly, should be an important factor in helping you to pass your test.

PERSONNEL ANALYST

KIND OF WORK

This is professional work in public personnel administration. Employees in this classification perform professional work in examination administration and test development and/or classification or compensation. Employees are expected to gain experience in the professional aspects of public personnel administration and as they progress are expected to handle responsible personnel assignments in an independent manner. Work may involve delegating work assignments to office support personnel. Work is subject to technical review by a professional superior at specified points during its progress and is subject to established timelines and standards for completion. Employees assist in the development of written exams and other complex selection devices through test validation studies; work with and interview incumbents and subject matter; perform related work as required.

SCOPE OF THE WRITTEN TEST

The written test will be designed to test for knowledge, skills, and/or abilities in such areas as:

1. Public personnel administration;
2. Classification and compensation;
3. Recruitment, selection and placement;
4. Preparing written material; and
5. Interviewing.

HOW TO TAKE A TEST

I. YOU MUST PASS AN EXAMINATION

A. WHAT EVERY CANDIDATE SHOULD KNOW

Examination applicants often ask us for help in preparing for the written test. What can I study in advance? What kinds of questions will be asked? How will the test be given? How will the papers be graded?

As an applicant for a civil service examination, you may be wondering about some of these things. Our purpose here is to suggest effective methods of advance study and to describe civil service examinations.

Your chances for success on this examination can be increased if you know how to prepare. Those "pre-examination jitters" can be reduced if you know what to expect. You can even experience an adventure in good citizenship if you know why civil service exams are given.

B. WHY ARE CIVIL SERVICE EXAMINATIONS GIVEN?

Civil service examinations are important to you in two ways. As a citizen, you want public jobs filled by employees who know how to do their work. As a job seeker, you want a fair chance to compete for that job on an equal footing with other candidates. The best-known means of accomplishing this two-fold goal is the competitive examination.

Exams are widely publicized throughout the nation. They may be administered for jobs in federal, state, city, municipal, town or village governments or agencies.

Any citizen may apply, with some limitations, such as the age or residence of applicants. Your experience and education may be reviewed to see whether you meet the requirements for the particular examination. When these requirements exist, they are reasonable and applied consistently to all applicants. Thus, a competitive examination may cause you some uneasiness now, but it is your privilege and safeguard.

C. HOW ARE CIVIL SERVICE EXAMS DEVELOPED?

Examinations are carefully written by trained technicians who are specialists in the field known as "psychological measurement," in consultation with recognized authorities in the field of work that the test will cover. These experts recommend the subject matter areas or skills to be tested; only those knowledges or skills important to your success on the job are included. The most reliable books and source materials available are used as references. Together, the experts and technicians judge the difficulty level of the questions.

Test technicians know how to phrase questions so that the problem is clearly stated. Their ethics do not permit "trick" or "catch" questions. Questions may have been tried out on sample groups, or subjected to statistical analysis, to determine their usefulness.

Written tests are often used in combination with performance tests, ratings of training and experience, and oral interviews. All of these measures combine to form the best-known means of finding the right person for the right job.

II. HOW TO PASS THE WRITTEN TEST

A. NATURE OF THE EXAMINATION

To prepare intelligently for civil service examinations, you should know how they differ from school examinations you have taken. In school you were assigned certain definite pages to read or subjects to cover. The examination questions were quite detailed and usually emphasized memory. Civil service exams, on the other hand, try to discover your present ability to perform the duties of a position, plus your potentiality to learn these duties. In other words, a civil service exam attempts to predict how successful you will be. Questions cover such a broad area that they cannot be as minute and detailed as school exam questions.

In the public service similar kinds of work, or positions, are grouped together in one "class." This process is known as *position-classification*. All the positions in a class are paid according to the salary range for that class. One class title covers all of these positions, and they are all tested by the same examination.

B. FOUR BASIC STEPS

1) Study the announcement

How, then, can you know what subjects to study? Our best answer is: "Learn as much as possible about the class of positions for which you've applied." The exam will test the knowledge, skills and abilities needed to do the work.

Your most valuable source of information about the position you want is the official exam announcement. This announcement lists the training and experience qualifications. Check these standards and apply only if you come reasonably close to meeting them.

The brief description of the position in the examination announcement offers some clues to the subjects which will be tested. Think about the job itself. Review the duties in your mind. Can you perform them, or are there some in which you are rusty? Fill in the blank spots in your preparation.

Many jurisdictions preview the written test in the exam announcement by including a section called "Knowledge and Abilities Required," "Scope of the Examination," or some similar heading. Here you will find out specifically what fields will be tested.

2) Review your own background

Once you learn in general what the position is all about, and what you need to know to do the work, ask yourself which subjects you already know fairly well and which need improvement. You may wonder whether to concentrate on improving your strong areas or on building some background in your fields of weakness. When the announcement has specified "some knowledge" or "considerable knowledge," or has used adjectives like "beginning principles of..." or "advanced ... methods," you can get a clue as to the number and difficulty of questions to be asked in any given field. More questions, and hence broader coverage, would be included for those subjects which are more important in the work. Now weigh your strengths and weaknesses against the job requirements and prepare accordingly.

3) Determine the level of the position

Another way to tell how intensively you should prepare is to understand the level of the job for which you are applying. Is it the entering level? In other words, is this the position in which beginners in a field of work are hired? Or is it an intermediate or advanced level? Sometimes this is indicated by such words as "Junior" or "Senior" in the class title. Other jurisdictions use Roman numerals to designate the level – Clerk I, Clerk II, for example. The word "Supervisor" sometimes appears in the title. If the level is not indicated by the title, check the description of duties. Will you be working under very close supervision, or will you have responsibility for independent decisions in this work?

4) Choose appropriate study materials

Now that you know the subjects to be examined and the relative amount of each subject to be covered, you can choose suitable study materials. For beginning level jobs, or even advanced ones, if you have a pronounced weakness in some aspect of your training, read a modern, standard textbook in that field. Be sure it is up to date and has general coverage. Such books are normally available at your library, and the librarian will be glad to help you locate one. For entry-level positions, questions of appropriate difficulty are chosen – neither highly advanced questions, nor those too simple. Such questions require careful thought but not advanced training.

If the position for which you are applying is technical or advanced, you will read more advanced, specialized material. If you are already familiar with the basic principles of your field, elementary textbooks would waste your time. Concentrate on advanced textbooks and technical periodicals. Think through the concepts and review difficult problems in your field.

These are all general sources. You can get more ideas on your own initiative, following these leads. For example, training manuals and publications of the government agency which employs workers in your field can be useful, particularly for technical and professional positions. A letter or visit to the government department involved may result in more specific study suggestions, and certainly will provide you with a more definite idea of the exact nature of the position you are seeking.

III. KINDS OF TESTS

Tests are used for purposes other than measuring knowledge and ability to perform specified duties. For some positions, it is equally important to test ability to make adjustments to new situations or to profit from training. In others, basic mental abilities not dependent on information are essential. Questions which test these things may not appear as pertinent to the duties of the position as those which test for knowledge and information. Yet they are often highly important parts of a fair examination. For very general questions, it is almost impossible to help you direct your study efforts. What we can do is to point out some of the more common of these general abilities needed in public service positions and describe some typical questions.

1) General information

Broad, general information has been found useful for predicting job success in some kinds of work. This is tested in a variety of ways, from vocabulary lists to questions about current events. Basic background in some field of work, such as sociology or economics, may be sampled in a group of questions. Often these are principles which have become familiar to most persons through exposure rather than through formal training. It is difficult to advise you how to study for these questions; being alert to the world around you is our best suggestion.

2) Verbal ability

An example of an ability needed in many positions is verbal or language ability. Verbal ability is, in brief, the ability to use and understand words. Vocabulary and grammar tests are typical measures of this ability. Reading comprehension or paragraph interpretation questions are common in many kinds of civil service tests. You are given a paragraph of written material and asked to find its central meaning.

3) Numerical ability

Number skills can be tested by the familiar arithmetic problem, by checking paired lists of numbers to see which are alike and which are different, or by interpreting charts and graphs. In the latter test, a graph may be printed in the test booklet which you are asked to use as the basis for answering questions.

4) Observation

A popular test for law-enforcement positions is the observation test. A picture is shown to you for several minutes, then taken away. Questions about the picture test your ability to observe both details and larger elements.

5) Following directions

In many positions in the public service, the employee must be able to carry out written instructions dependably and accurately. You may be given a chart with several columns, each column listing a variety of information. The questions require you to carry out directions involving the information given in the chart.

6) Skills and aptitudes

Performance tests effectively measure some manual skills and aptitudes. When the skill is one in which you are trained, such as typing or shorthand, you can practice. These tests are often very much like those given in business school or high school courses. For many of the other skills and aptitudes, however, no short-time preparation can be made. Skills and abilities natural to you or that you have developed throughout your lifetime are being tested.

Many of the general questions just described provide all the data needed to answer the questions and ask you to use your reasoning ability to find the answers. Your best preparation for these tests, as well as for tests of facts and ideas, is to be at your physical and mental best. You, no doubt, have your own methods of getting into an exam-taking mood and keeping "in shape." The next section lists some ideas on this subject.

IV. KINDS OF QUESTIONS

Only rarely is the "essay" question, which you answer in narrative form, used in civil service tests. Civil service tests are usually of the short-answer type. Full instructions for answering these questions will be given to you at the examination. But in case this is your first experience with short-answer questions and separate answer sheets, here is what you need to know:

1) Multiple-choice Questions

Most popular of the short-answer questions is the "multiple choice" or "best answer" question. It can be used, for example, to test for factual knowledge, ability to solve problems or judgment in meeting situations found at work.

A multiple-choice question is normally one of three types—

- It can begin with an incomplete statement followed by several possible endings. You are to find the one ending which *best* completes the statement, although some of the others may not be entirely wrong.
- It can also be a complete statement in the form of a question which is answered by choosing one of the statements listed.

- It can be in the form of a problem – again you select the best answer.

Here is an example of a multiple-choice question with a discussion which should give you some clues as to the method for choosing the right answer:

> When an employee has a complaint about his assignment, the action which will *best* help him overcome his difficulty is to
> A. discuss his difficulty with his coworkers
> B. take the problem to the head of the organization
> C. take the problem to the person who gave him the assignment
> D. say nothing to anyone about his complaint

In answering this question, you should study each of the choices to find which is best. Consider choice "A" – Certainly an employee may discuss his complaint with fellow employees, but no change or improvement can result, and the complaint remains unresolved. Choice "B" is a poor choice since the head of the organization probably does not know what assignment you have been given, and taking your problem to him is known as "going over the head" of the supervisor. The supervisor, or person who made the assignment, is the person who can clarify it or correct any injustice. Choice "C" is, therefore, correct. To say nothing, as in choice "D," is unwise. Supervisors have and interest in knowing the problems employees are facing, and the employee is seeking a solution to his problem.

2) True/False Questions

The "true/false" or "right/wrong" form of question is sometimes used. Here a complete statement is given. Your job is to decide whether the statement is right or wrong.

SAMPLE: A roaming cell-phone call to a nearby city costs less than a non-roaming call to a distant city.

This statement is wrong, or false, since roaming calls are more expensive.

This is not a complete list of all possible question forms, although most of the others are variations of these common types. You will always get complete directions for answering questions. Be sure you understand *how* to mark your answers – ask questions until you do.

V. RECORDING YOUR ANSWERS

Computer terminals are used more and more today for many different kinds of exams.

For an examination with very few applicants, you may be told to record your answers in the test booklet itself. Separate answer sheets are much more common. If this separate answer sheet is to be scored by machine – and this is often the case – it is highly important that you mark your answers correctly in order to get credit.

An electronic scoring machine is often used in civil service offices because of the speed with which papers can be scored. Machine-scored answer sheets must be marked with a pencil, which will be given to you. This pencil has a high graphite content which responds to the electronic scoring machine. As a matter of fact, stray dots may register as answers, so do not let your pencil rest on the answer sheet while you are pondering the correct answer. Also, if your pencil lead breaks or is otherwise defective, ask for another.

Since the answer sheet will be dropped in a slot in the scoring machine, be careful not to bend the corners or get the paper crumpled.

The answer sheet normally has five vertical columns of numbers, with 30 numbers to a column. These numbers correspond to the question numbers in your test booklet. After each number, going across the page are four or five pairs of dotted lines. These short dotted lines have small letters or numbers above them. The first two pairs may also have a "T" or "F" above the letters. This indicates that the first two pairs only are to be used if the questions are of the true-false type. If the questions are multiple choice, disregard the "T" and "F" and pay attention only to the small letters or numbers.

Answer your questions in the manner of the sample that follows:

32. The largest city in the United States is
    A. Washington, D.C.
    B. New York City
    C. Chicago
    D. Detroit
    E. San Francisco

1) Choose the answer you think is best. (New York City is the largest, so "B" is correct.)
2) Find the row of dotted lines numbered the same as the question you are answering. (Find row number 32)
3) Find the pair of dotted lines corresponding to the answer. (Find the pair of lines under the mark "B.")
4) Make a solid black mark between the dotted lines.

VI. BEFORE THE TEST

Common sense will help you find procedures to follow to get ready for an examination. Too many of us, however, overlook these sensible measures. Indeed, nervousness and fatigue have been found to be the most serious reasons why applicants fail to do their best on civil service tests. Here is a list of reminders:

- Begin your preparation early – Don't wait until the last minute to go scurrying around for books and materials or to find out what the position is all about.
- Prepare continuously – An hour a night for a week is better than an all-night cram session. This has been definitely established. What is more, a night a week for a month will return better dividends than crowding your study into a shorter period of time.
- Locate the place of the exam – You have been sent a notice telling you when and where to report for the examination. If the location is in a different town or otherwise unfamiliar to you, it would be well to inquire the best route and learn something about the building.
- Relax the night before the test – Allow your mind to rest. Do not study at all that night. Plan some mild recreation or diversion; then go to bed early and get a good night's sleep.
- Get up early enough to make a leisurely trip to the place for the test – This way unforeseen events, traffic snarls, unfamiliar buildings, etc. will not upset you.
- Dress comfortably – A written test is not a fashion show. You will be known by number and not by name, so wear something comfortable.

- Leave excess paraphernalia at home – Shopping bags and odd bundles will get in your way. You need bring only the items mentioned in the official notice you received; usually everything you need is provided. Do not bring reference books to the exam. They will only confuse those last minutes and be taken away from you when in the test room.
- Arrive somewhat ahead of time – If because of transportation schedules you must get there very early, bring a newspaper or magazine to take your mind off yourself while waiting.
- Locate the examination room – When you have found the proper room, you will be directed to the seat or part of the room where you will sit. Sometimes you are given a sheet of instructions to read while you are waiting. Do not fill out any forms until you are told to do so; just read them and be prepared.
- Relax and prepare to listen to the instructions
- If you have any physical problem that may keep you from doing your best, be sure to tell the test administrator. If you are sick or in poor health, you really cannot do your best on the exam. You can come back and take the test some other time.

VII. AT THE TEST

The day of the test is here and you have the test booklet in your hand. The temptation to get going is very strong. Caution! There is more to success than knowing the right answers. You must know how to identify your papers and understand variations in the type of short-answer question used in this particular examination. Follow these suggestions for maximum results from your efforts:

1) Cooperate with the monitor

The test administrator has a duty to create a situation in which you can be as much at ease as possible. He will give instructions, tell you when to begin, check to see that you are marking your answer sheet correctly, and so on. He is not there to guard you, although he will see that your competitors do not take unfair advantage. He wants to help you do your best.

2) Listen to all instructions

Don't jump the gun! Wait until you understand all directions. In most civil service tests you get more time than you need to answer the questions. So don't be in a hurry. Read each word of instructions until you clearly understand the meaning. Study the examples, listen to all announcements and follow directions. Ask questions if you do not understand what to do.

3) Identify your papers

Civil service exams are usually identified by number only. You will be assigned a number; you must not put your name on your test papers. Be sure to copy your number correctly. Since more than one exam may be given, copy your exact examination title.

4) Plan your time

Unless you are told that a test is a "speed" or "rate of work" test, speed itself is usually not important. Time enough to answer all the questions will be provided, but this does not mean that you have all day. An overall time limit has been set. Divide the total time (in minutes) by the number of questions to determine the approximate time you have for each question.

5) Do not linger over difficult questions

If you come across a difficult question, mark it with a paper clip (useful to have along) and come back to it when you have been through the booklet. One caution if you do this – be sure to skip a number on your answer sheet as well. Check often to be sure that you have not lost your place and that you are marking in the row numbered the same as the question you are answering.

6) Read the questions

Be sure you know what the question asks! Many capable people are unsuccessful because they failed to *read* the questions correctly.

7) Answer all questions

Unless you have been instructed that a penalty will be deducted for incorrect answers, it is better to guess than to omit a question.

8) Speed tests

It is often better NOT to guess on speed tests. It has been found that on timed tests people are tempted to spend the last few seconds before time is called in marking answers at random – without even reading them – in the hope of picking up a few extra points. To discourage this practice, the instructions may warn you that your score will be "corrected" for guessing. That is, a penalty will be applied. The incorrect answers will be deducted from the correct ones, or some other penalty formula will be used.

9) Review your answers

If you finish before time is called, go back to the questions you guessed or omitted to give them further thought. Review other answers if you have time.

10) Return your test materials

If you are ready to leave before others have finished or time is called, take ALL your materials to the monitor and leave quietly. Never take any test material with you. The monitor can discover whose papers are not complete, and taking a test booklet may be grounds for disqualification.

VIII. EXAMINATION TECHNIQUES

1) Read the general instructions carefully. These are usually printed on the first page of the exam booklet. As a rule, these instructions refer to the timing of the examination; the fact that you should not start work until the signal and must stop work at a signal, etc. If there are any *special* instructions, such as a choice of questions to be answered, make sure that you note this instruction carefully.

2) When you are ready to start work on the examination, that is as soon as the signal has been given, read the instructions to each question booklet, underline any key words or phrases, such as *least, best, outline, describe* and the like. In this way you will tend to answer as requested rather than discover on reviewing your paper that you *listed without describing*, that you selected the *worst* choice rather than the *best* choice, etc.

3) If the examination is of the objective or multiple-choice type – that is, each question will also give a series of possible answers: A, B, C or D, and you are called upon to select the best answer and write the letter next to that answer on your answer paper – it is advisable to start answering each question in turn. There may be anywhere from 50 to 100 such questions in the three or four hours allotted and you can see how much time would be taken if you read through all the questions before beginning to answer any. Furthermore, if you come across a question or group of questions which you know would be difficult to answer, it would undoubtedly affect your handling of all the other questions.

4) If the examination is of the essay type and contains but a few questions, it is a moot point as to whether you should read all the questions before starting to answer any one. Of course, if you are given a choice – say five out of seven and the like – then it is essential to read all the questions so you can eliminate the two that are most difficult. If, however, you are asked to answer all the questions, there may be danger in trying to answer the easiest one first because you may find that you will spend too much time on it. The best technique is to answer the first question, then proceed to the second, etc.

5) Time your answers. Before the exam begins, write down the time it started, then add the time allowed for the examination and write down the time it must be completed, then divide the time available somewhat as follows:
    - If 3-1/2 hours are allowed, that would be 210 minutes. If you have 80 objective-type questions, that would be an average of 2-1/2 minutes per question. Allow yourself no more than 2 minutes per question, or a total of 160 minutes, which will permit about 50 minutes to review.
    - If for the time allotment of 210 minutes there are 7 essay questions to answer, that would average about 30 minutes a question. Give yourself only 25 minutes per question so that you have about 35 minutes to review.

6) The most important instruction is to *read each question* and make sure you know what is wanted. The second most important instruction is to *time yourself properly* so that you answer every question. The third most important instruction is to *answer every question*. Guess if you have to but include something for each question. Remember that you will receive no credit for a blank and will probably receive some credit if you write something in answer to an essay question. If you guess a letter – say "B" for a multiple-choice question – you may have guessed right. If you leave a blank as an answer to a multiple-choice question, the examiners may respect your feelings but it will not add a point to your score. Some exams may penalize you for wrong answers, so in such cases *only*, you may not want to guess unless you have some basis for your answer.

7) Suggestions
    a. Objective-type questions
        1. Examine the question booklet for proper sequence of pages and questions
        2. Read all instructions carefully
        3. Skip any question which seems too difficult; return to it after all other questions have been answered
        4. Apportion your time properly; do not spend too much time on any single question or group of questions

5. Note and underline key words – *all, most, fewest, least, best, worst, same, opposite,* etc.
6. Pay particular attention to negatives
7. Note unusual option, e.g., unduly long, short, complex, different or similar in content to the body of the question
8. Observe the use of "hedging" words – *probably, may, most likely,* etc.
9. Make sure that your answer is put next to the same number as the question
10. Do not second-guess unless you have good reason to believe the second answer is definitely more correct
11. Cross out original answer if you decide another answer is more accurate; do not erase until you are ready to hand your paper in
12. Answer all questions; guess unless instructed otherwise
13. Leave time for review

b. Essay questions
1. Read each question carefully
2. Determine exactly what is wanted. Underline key words or phrases.
3. Decide on outline or paragraph answer
4. Include many different points and elements unless asked to develop any one or two points or elements
5. Show impartiality by giving pros and cons unless directed to select one side only
6. Make and write down any assumptions you find necessary to answer the questions
7. Watch your English, grammar, punctuation and choice of words
8. Time your answers; don't crowd material

8) Answering the essay question

Most essay questions can be answered by framing the specific response around several key words or ideas. Here are a few such key words or ideas:

M's: manpower, materials, methods, money, management
P's: purpose, program, policy, plan, procedure, practice, problems, pitfalls, personnel, public relations

a. Six basic steps in handling problems:
1. Preliminary plan and background development
2. Collect information, data and facts
3. Analyze and interpret information, data and facts
4. Analyze and develop solutions as well as make recommendations
5. Prepare report and sell recommendations
6. Install recommendations and follow up effectiveness

b. Pitfalls to avoid
1. *Taking things for granted* – A statement of the situation does not necessarily imply that each of the elements is necessarily true; for example, a complaint may be invalid and biased so that all that can be taken for granted is that a complaint has been registered

2. *Considering only one side of a situation* – Wherever possible, indicate several alternatives and then point out the reasons you selected the best one
3. *Failing to indicate follow up* – Whenever your answer indicates action on your part, make certain that you will take proper follow-up action to see how successful your recommendations, procedures or actions turn out to be
4. *Taking too long in answering any single question* – Remember to time your answers properly

IX. AFTER THE TEST

Scoring procedures differ in detail among civil service jurisdictions although the general principles are the same. Whether the papers are hand-scored or graded by machine we have described, they are nearly always graded by number. That is, the person who marks the paper knows only the number – never the name – of the applicant. Not until all the papers have been graded will they be matched with names. If other tests, such as training and experience or oral interview ratings have been given, scores will be combined. Different parts of the examination usually have different weights. For example, the written test might count 60 percent of the final grade, and a rating of training and experience 40 percent. In many jurisdictions, veterans will have a certain number of points added to their grades.

After the final grade has been determined, the names are placed in grade order and an eligible list is established. There are various methods for resolving ties between those who get the same final grade – probably the most common is to place first the name of the person whose application was received first. Job offers are made from the eligible list in the order the names appear on it. You will be notified of your grade and your rank as soon as all these computations have been made. This will be done as rapidly as possible.

People who are found to meet the requirements in the announcement are called "eligibles." Their names are put on a list of eligible candidates. An eligible's chances of getting a job depend on how high he stands on this list and how fast agencies are filling jobs from the list.

When a job is to be filled from a list of eligibles, the agency asks for the names of people on the list of eligibles for that job. When the civil service commission receives this request, it sends to the agency the names of the three people highest on this list. Or, if the job to be filled has specialized requirements, the office sends the agency the names of the top three persons who meet these requirements from the general list.

The appointing officer makes a choice from among the three people whose names were sent to him. If the selected person accepts the appointment, the names of the others are put back on the list to be considered for future openings.

That is the rule in hiring from all kinds of eligible lists, whether they are for typist, carpenter, chemist, or something else. For every vacancy, the appointing officer has his choice of any one of the top three eligibles on the list. This explains why the person whose name is on top of the list sometimes does not get an appointment when some of the persons lower on the list do. If the appointing officer chooses the second or third eligible, the No. 1 eligible does not get a job at once, but stays on the list until he is appointed or the list is terminated.

X. HOW TO PASS THE INTERVIEW TEST

The examination for which you applied requires an oral interview test. You have already taken the written test and you are now being called for the interview test – the final part of the formal examination.

You may think that it is not possible to prepare for an interview test and that there are no procedures to follow during an interview. Our purpose is to point out some things you can do in advance that will help you and some good rules to follow and pitfalls to avoid while you are being interviewed.

What is an interview supposed to test?

The written examination is designed to test the technical knowledge and competence of the candidate; the oral is designed to evaluate intangible qualities, not readily measured otherwise, and to establish a list showing the relative fitness of each candidate – as measured against his competitors – for the position sought. Scoring is not on the basis of "right" and "wrong," but on a sliding scale of values ranging from "not passable" to "outstanding." As a matter of fact, it is possible to achieve a relatively low score without a single "incorrect" answer because of evident weakness in the qualities being measured.

Occasionally, an examination may consist entirely of an oral test – either an individual or a group oral. In such cases, information is sought concerning the technical knowledges and abilities of the candidate, since there has been no written examination for this purpose. More commonly, however, an oral test is used to supplement a written examination.

Who conducts interviews?

The composition of oral boards varies among different jurisdictions. In nearly all, a representative of the personnel department serves as chairman. One of the members of the board may be a representative of the department in which the candidate would work. In some cases, "outside experts" are used, and, frequently, a businessman or some other representative of the general public is asked to serve. Labor and management or other special groups may be represented. The aim is to secure the services of experts in the appropriate field.

However the board is composed, it is a good idea (and not at all improper or unethical) to ascertain in advance of the interview who the members are and what groups they represent. When you are introduced to them, you will have some idea of their backgrounds and interests, and at least you will not stutter and stammer over their names.

What should be done before the interview?

While knowledge about the board members is useful and takes some of the surprise element out of the interview, there is other preparation which is more substantive. It *is* possible to prepare for an oral interview – in several ways:

1) Keep a copy of your application and review it carefully before the interview

This may be the only document before the oral board, and the starting point of the interview. Know what education and experience you have listed there, and the sequence and dates of all of it. Sometimes the board will ask you to review the highlights of your experience for them; you should not have to hem and haw doing it.

2) Study the class specification and the examination announcement

Usually, the oral board has one or both of these to guide them. The qualities, characteristics or knowledges required by the position sought are stated in these documents. They offer valuable clues as to the nature of the oral interview. For example, if the job involves supervisory responsibilities, the announcement will usually indicate that knowledge of modern supervisory methods and the qualifications of the candidate as a supervisor will be tested. If so, you can expect such questions, frequently in the form of a hypothetical situation which you are expected to solve. NEVER go into an oral without knowledge of the duties and responsibilities of the job you seek.

3) Think through each qualification required

Try to visualize the kind of questions you would ask if you were a board member. How well could you answer them? Try especially to appraise your own knowledge and background in each area, *measured against the job sought*, and identify any areas in which you are weak. Be critical and realistic – do not flatter yourself.

4) Do some general reading in areas in which you feel you may be weak

For example, if the job involves supervision and your past experience has NOT, some general reading in supervisory methods and practices, particularly in the field of human relations, might be useful. Do NOT study agency procedures or detailed manuals. The oral board will be testing your understanding and capacity, not your memory.

5) Get a good night's sleep and watch your general health and mental attitude

You will want a clear head at the interview. Take care of a cold or any other minor ailment, and of course, no hangovers.

What should be done on the day of the interview?

Now comes the day of the interview itself. Give yourself plenty of time to get there. Plan to arrive somewhat ahead of the scheduled time, particularly if your appointment is in the fore part of the day. If a previous candidate fails to appear, the board might be ready for you a bit early. By early afternoon an oral board is almost invariably behind schedule if there are many candidates, and you may have to wait. Take along a book or magazine to read, or your application to review, but leave any extraneous material in the waiting room when you go in for your interview. In any event, relax and compose yourself.

The matter of dress is important. The board is forming impressions about you – from your experience, your manners, your attitude, and your appearance. Give your personal appearance careful attention. Dress your best, but not your flashiest. Choose conservative, appropriate clothing, and be sure it is immaculate. This is a business interview, and your appearance should indicate that you regard it as such. Besides, being well groomed and properly dressed will help boost your confidence.

Sooner or later, someone will call your name and escort you into the interview room. *This is it.* From here on you are on your own. It is too late for any more preparation. But remember, you asked for this opportunity to prove your fitness, and you are here because your request was granted.

What happens when you go in?

The usual sequence of events will be as follows: The clerk (who is often the board stenographer) will introduce you to the chairman of the oral board, who will introduce you to the other members of the board. Acknowledge the introductions before you sit down. Do not be surprised if you find a microphone facing you or a stenotypist sitting by. Oral interviews are usually recorded in the event of an appeal or other review.

Usually the chairman of the board will open the interview by reviewing the highlights of your education and work experience from your application – primarily for the benefit of the other members of the board, as well as to get the material into the record. Do not interrupt or comment unless there is an error or significant misinterpretation; if that is the case, do not hesitate. But do not quibble about insignificant matters. Also, he will usually ask you some question about your education, experience or your present job – partly to get you to start talking and to establish the interviewing "rapport." He may start the actual questioning, or turn it over to one of the other members. Frequently, each member undertakes the questioning on a particular area, one in which he is perhaps most competent, so you can expect each member to participate in the examination. Because time is limited, you may also expect some rather abrupt switches in the direction the questioning takes, so do not be upset by it. Normally, a board member will not pursue a single line of questioning unless he discovers a particular strength or weakness.

After each member has participated, the chairman will usually ask whether any member has any further questions, then will ask you if you have anything you wish to add. Unless you are expecting this question, it may floor you. Worse, it may start you off on an extended, extemporaneous speech. The board is not usually seeking more information. The question is principally to offer you a last opportunity to present further qualifications or to indicate that you have nothing to add. So, if you feel that a significant qualification or characteristic has been overlooked, it is proper to point it out in a sentence or so. Do not compliment the board on the thoroughness of their examination – they have been sketchy, and you know it. If you wish, merely say, "No thank you, I have nothing further to add." This is a point where you can "talk yourself out" of a good impression or fail to present an important bit of information. Remember, *you close the interview yourself.*

The chairman will then say, "That is all, Mr. ______, thank you." Do not be startled; the interview is over, and quicker than you think. Thank him, gather your belongings and take your leave. Save your sigh of relief for the other side of the door.

How to put your best foot forward

Throughout this entire process, you may feel that the board individually and collectively is trying to pierce your defenses, seek out your hidden weaknesses and embarrass and confuse you. Actually, this is not true. They are obliged to make an appraisal of your qualifications for the job you are seeking, and they want to see you in your best light. Remember, they must interview all candidates and a non-cooperative candidate may become a failure in spite of their best efforts to bring out his qualifications. Here are 15 suggestions that will help you:

1) Be natural – Keep your attitude confident, not cocky

If you are not confident that you can do the job, do not expect the board to be. Do not apologize for your weaknesses, try to bring out your strong points. The board is interested in a positive, not negative, presentation. Cockiness will antagonize any board member and make him wonder if you are covering up a weakness by a false show of strength.

2) Get comfortable, but don't lounge or sprawl

Sit erectly but not stiffly. A careless posture may lead the board to conclude that you are careless in other things, or at least that you are not impressed by the importance of the occasion. Either conclusion is natural, even if incorrect. Do not fuss with your clothing, a pencil or an ashtray. Your hands may occasionally be useful to emphasize a point; do not let them become a point of distraction.

3) Do not wisecrack or make small talk

This is a serious situation, and your attitude should show that you consider it as such. Further, the time of the board is limited – they do not want to waste it, and neither should you.

4) Do not exaggerate your experience or abilities

In the first place, from information in the application or other interviews and sources, the board may know more about you than you think. Secondly, you probably will not get away with it. An experienced board is rather adept at spotting such a situation, so do not take the chance.

5) If you know a board member, do not make a point of it, yet do not hide it

Certainly you are not fooling him, and probably not the other members of the board. Do not try to take advantage of your acquaintanceship – it will probably do you little good.

6) Do not dominate the interview

Let the board do that. They will give you the clues – do not assume that you have to do all the talking. Realize that the board has a number of questions to ask you, and do not try to take up all the interview time by showing off your extensive knowledge of the answer to the first one.

7) Be attentive

You only have 20 minutes or so, and you should keep your attention at its sharpest throughout. When a member is addressing a problem or question to you, give him your undivided attention. Address your reply principally to him, but do not exclude the other board members.

8) Do not interrupt

A board member may be stating a problem for you to analyze. He will ask you a question when the time comes. Let him state the problem, and wait for the question.

9) Make sure you understand the question

Do not try to answer until you are sure what the question is. If it is not clear, restate it in your own words or ask the board member to clarify it for you. However, do not haggle about minor elements.

10) Reply promptly but not hastily

A common entry on oral board rating sheets is "candidate responded readily," or "candidate hesitated in replies." Respond as promptly and quickly as you can, but do not jump to a hasty, ill-considered answer.

11) Do not be peremptory in your answers

A brief answer is proper – but do not fire your answer back. That is a losing game from your point of view. The board member can probably ask questions much faster than you can answer them.

12) Do not try to create the answer you think the board member wants

He is interested in what kind of mind you have and how it works – not in playing games. Furthermore, he can usually spot this practice and will actually grade you down on it.

13) Do not switch sides in your reply merely to agree with a board member

Frequently, a member will take a contrary position merely to draw you out and to see if you are willing and able to defend your point of view. Do not start a debate, yet do not surrender a good position. If a position is worth taking, it is worth defending.

14) Do not be afraid to admit an error in judgment if you are shown to be wrong

The board knows that you are forced to reply without any opportunity for careful consideration. Your answer may be demonstrably wrong. If so, admit it and get on with the interview.

15) Do not dwell at length on your present job

The opening question may relate to your present assignment. Answer the question but do not go into an extended discussion. You are being examined for a *new* job, not your present one. As a matter of fact, try to phrase ALL your answers in terms of the job for which you are being examined.

Basis of Rating

Probably you will forget most of these "do's" and "don'ts" when you walk into the oral interview room. Even remembering them all will not ensure you a passing grade. Perhaps you did not have the qualifications in the first place. But remembering them will help you to put your best foot forward, without treading on the toes of the board members.

Rumor and popular opinion to the contrary notwithstanding, an oral board wants you to make the best appearance possible. They know you are under pressure – but they also want to see how you respond to it as a guide to what your reaction would be under the pressures of the job you seek. They will be influenced by the degree of poise you display, the personal traits you show and the manner in which you respond.

ABOUT THIS BOOK

This book contains tests divided into Examination Sections. Go through each test, answering every question in the margin. We have also attached a sample answer sheet at the back of the book that can be removed and used. At the end of each test look at the answer key and check your answers. On the ones you got wrong, look at the right answer choice and learn. Do not fill in the answers first. Do not memorize the questions and answers, but understand the answer and principles involved. On your test, the questions will likely be different from the samples. Questions are changed and new ones added. If you understand these past questions you should have success with any changes that arise. Tests may consist of several types of questions. We have additional books on each subject should more study be advisable or necessary for you. Finally, the more you study, the better prepared you will be. This book is intended to be the last thing you study before you walk into the examination room. Prior study of relevant texts is also recommended. NLC publishes some of these in our Fundamental Series. Knowledge and good sense are important factors in passing your exam. Good luck also helps. So now study this Passbook, absorb the material contained within and take that knowledge into the examination. Then do your best to pass that exam.

EXAMINATION SECTION

EXAMINATION SECTION

TEST 1

DIRECTIONS: Each question or incomplete statement is followed by several suggested answers or completions. Select the one that BEST answers the question or completes the statement. *PRINT THE LETTER OF THE CORRECT ANSWER IN THE SPACE AT THE RIGHT.*

1. Assume that a civil service list has been established for a position in an agency which had provisional appointees serving in three permanent vacancies. One of these provisionals is on the eligible list, but was discharged because permanent appointments were accepted by three eligibles who were higher on the list. The former provisional has complained to the agency head, alleging that special efforts were made to appoint these eligible. The personnel officer of the agency should advise the agency head that 1.____
   A. the court could compel them to appoint the former provisional appointee
   B. he is required by civil service law to appoint the higher ranking eligibles from the list
   C. the human rights commission could compel him to appoint the former provisional appointee
   D. he should attempt conciliation

2. Assume that two accountants working in a section under your supervision were appointed from the same eligible list. Accountant Jones received a higher score on the competitive examination than Accountant Doe; Jones was third on the eligible list and Doe was fifth. Jones was told to report to work on March 15 but Doe, who was working under a provisional appointment, was given permanent status as of March 1. For economic reasons, your agency head is considering abolishing one position of accountant and requests guidance from you before making any decision. 2.____
   It would be BEST to tell him that
   A. if he decides to abolish one position of accountant, he should lay off Jones because Doe was given permanent status before Jones
   B. under the rule of *one in three*, Doe could not have been reached for appointment before Jones, so that Doe would have to be laid off first
   C. if he decides to abolish one position of accountant, he should lay off Doe because Doe's provisional appointment was in violation of the Civil Service Law
   D. he should evaluate the performance of Jones and Doe before making any determination as to which accountant to lay off

3. An employee who has been on the job for a number of years became a problem drinker during the past year. The supervisor and this employee are good friends. 3.____
   Because this problem has been affecting the work of the unit adversely, it would be BEST for the supervisor to

A. attempt to cover up the problem by moving the subordinate's desk to a corner of the office where he would not be noticed so readily
B. refer the employee for counseling to the employee counseling service
C. reassign some of the problem drinker's responsibilities to other employees
D. send the employee home in a tactful manner whenever he reports for duty in an unfit condition

4. In a strike situation, a member of the striking union reports for work but abstains from the full performance of his duties in his normal manner. 4.____
According to the state civil service law, it is ACCURATE to say that the
A. employee should be presumed to have engaged in a strike
B. employee should not be presumed to have engaged in a strike
C. city must bear the burden of proving that the employee engaged in a strike
D. city may deny the employee the opportunity to rebut any charge that he engaged in a strike

5. Assume that, as a manager in a health agency which is establishing a *management-by-objective* program, you are asked to review and make recommendations on the following goals set by the agency head for the coming year. 5.____
Which one of these objectives should you recommend dropping because of difficulty in verifying the degree to which the goal has been attained?
A. Establishing night clinics in two preventive health care centers
B. Informing more people of available health services
C. Preparing a training manual for data-processing personnel
D. Producing a 4-page health news bulletin to be distributed monthly to employees

6. The MAIN purpose of the *management-by-objectives* system is to 6.____
A. develop a method of appraising the performance of managerial employees against verifiable objectives rather than against subjective appraisals and personal supervision
B. decentralize managerial decision-making more effectively by setting goals for personnel all the way down to each first-line supervisor as well as to staff people
C. increase managerial accountability and improve managerial effectiveness
D. enable top level managerial employees to impose quantitative goals which will focus attention on the relevant trends that may affect the future

7. Certain city and state employees are on one year's probation for violating the strike provisions of the state civil service law. 7.____
According to a ruling by the state attorney general, in the event of layoffs during their year of probation, the status of these employees should be considered
A. *permanent*, with retention rights based on original date of appointment
B. *probationary*, subject to layoff before permanent employees

C. *permanent*, to be credited with one year less service than indicated by the original date of appointment
D. *probationary*, subject to layoff before other employees in the layoff unit except for those with one year's seniority

8. Assume that, as a senior supervisor conducting a training course for a group of newly assigned first-line supervisors, you emphasize that an effective supervisor should encourage employee suggestions. One member of the group dissents, asserting that many employees come up with worthless, time-wasting ideas. 8.____
The one of the following which would be the MOST appropriate response for you to make is that
A. the supervisor's attitude is wrong, because no suggestion is entirely without merit
B. the supervisor must remember that encouragement of employee suggestions is the major part of any employee development program
C. even if a suggestion seems worthless, the participation of the employee helps to increase his identification with the agency
D. even if a suggestion seems worthless, the supervisor may be able to save it for future use

9. The *grapevine* is an informal channel of communication which exists among employees in an organization as a natural result of their social interaction, and their desire to be kept posted on the latest information. Some information transmitted through the grapevine is truth, some half-truth, and some just rumor. 9.____
Which one of the following would be the MOST appropriate attitude for a member of a management team to have about the grapevine?
A. The grapevine often carries false, malicious, and uncontrollable rumors and management should try to stamp it out by improving official channels of communication.
B. There are more important problems; normally only a small percentage of employees are interested in information transmitted through the grapevine.
C. The grapevine can give management insight into what employees think and feel and can help to supplement the formal communication systems.
D. The grapevine gives employees a harmless outlet for their imagination and an opportunity to relieve their fears and tensions in the form of rumors.

10. Although there are no formal performance appraisal mechanisms for non-managerial employees, managers nevertheless make informal appraisals because some method is needed to measure progress and to let employees know how they are doing. 10.____
The MOST import recent trend in making performance appraisals is toward judging the employee primarily on the extent to which he has
A. tried to perform his assigned tasks
B. demonstrated personal traits which are accepted as necessary to do the job satisfactorily

C. accomplished the objectives set for his job
D. followed the procedures established for the job

11. The proof of a successful human relations program in an organization is the morale crises that never happen. 11.____
Of the following, the implication for managers that follows MOST directly from this statement is that they should
A. review and initiate revisions in all organization policies which may have an adverse effect on employee morale
B. place more emphasis on ability to anticipate and prevent morale problems than on ability to resolve an actual crisis
C. see that first-line supervisors work fairly and understandingly with employees
D. avoid morale crises at all costs, since even the best resolution leaves scar, suspicions, and animosities

12. Suppose that you are conducting a conference on a specific problem. One employee makes a suggestion which you think is highly impractical. 12.____
Of the following, the way for you to respond to this suggestion is FIRST to
A. be frank and tell the employee that his solution is wrong
B. ask the employee in what way his suggestion will solve the problem under discussion
C. refrain from any comment on it, and ask the group whether they have any other solutions to offer
D. ask another participant to point out what is wrong with the suggestion

13. Suppose that a manager notices continuing deterioration in the work, conduct, and interpersonal relationships of one of his immediate subordinates, indicating that this employee has more than a minor emotional problem. Although the manager has made an attempt to help this employee by talking over his problems with him on several occasions, the employee has shown little improvement. 13.____
Of the following, generally the MOST constructive action for the manager to take at this point would be to
A. continue to be supportive by sympathetic listening and counseling
B. show tolerance toward the performance of the disturbed employee
C. discuss the employee's deteriorating condition with him and suggest that he seek professional help
D. consider whether the need of this employee and the agency would be best served by his transfer to another division

14. A manager has a problem involving conflict between two employees concerning a method of performing a work assignment. He does not know the reasons for this conflict. 14.____
The MOST valuable communications method he can use to aid him in resolving the problem is
A. a formal hearing for each employee
B. a staff meeting

C. disciplinary memoranda
D. an informal interview with each employee

15. As a training technique, role-playing is generally considered to be MOST successful when it results in 15.____
A. uncovering the underlying causes of conflict so that any recurrences are prevented
B. recreating an actual work situation which involves conflict among people and in which members of the group simulate specific personalities
C. freeing some people from patterns of rigid thinking and enabling them to look at themselves and others in a new way
D. increasing the participants' powers of logic and reasoning

16. In conducting a disciplinary interview, a supervisor finds that he must ask some highly personal questions which are relevant to the problem at hand. 16.____
The interviewer is MOST likely to get truthful answers to these questions if he asks them
A. early in the interview, before the interviewee has had a chance to become emotional
B. in a manner so that the interviewee can answer them with a simple *yes* or *no*
C. well into the interview, after rapport and trust have been established
D. just after the close of the interview, so that the questions appear to be off the record

17. Suppose that, as a newly assigned manager, you observe that a supervisor in your division uses autocratic methods which are causing resentment among his subordinates. 17.____
Of the following, the MOST likely reason for this supervisor's using such methods is that he
A. was probably exposed to this type of supervision himself
B. does not have an intuitive sense of tact, diplomacy, and consideration and no amount of training can change this
C. received approval for use of such method from his former subordinates
D. does not understand the basic concept of rewards and punishment in the practice of supervision

18. A newly appointed employee, Mr. Jones, was added to the staff of a supervisor who, because of the pressure of other work, turned him over to an experienced subordinate by saying, *Show Mr. Jones around and give him something to do.* 18.____
On the basis of this experience, Mr. Jones' FIRST impression of his new position was most likely to have been
A. *negative*, mainly because it appeared that his job was not worth his supervisor's attention
B. *negative*, mainly because the more experienced subordinate would tend to emphasize the unpleasant aspects of the work
C. *positive*, mainly because his supervisor wasted no time in assigning him to a subordinate
D. *positive*, mainly because he saw himself working for a dynamic supervisor who expected immediate results

19. An employee who stays in one assignment for a number of years often develops a feeling of possessiveness concerning his knowledge of the job which may develop into a problem. 19.____
Of the following, the BEST way for a supervisor to remedy this difficulty is to
   A. give the employee less important work to do
   B. point out minor errors as often as possible
   C. raise performance standards for all employees
   D. rotate the employee to a different assignment

20. A supervisor who tends to be supportive of his subordinates, in contrast to a supervisor who relies upon an authoritarian style of leadership, is more likely, in dealing with his staff, to have to listen to complaints, to have to tolerate emotionally upset employees, and even have to hear unreasonable and insulting remarks. 20.____
Compared to the authoritarian supervisor, he is MORE likely to
   A. be unconsciously fearful of failure
   B. have an overriding interest in production
   C. have subordinates who are better educated
   D. receive accurate feedback information

KEY (CORRECT ANSWERS)

1.	B	11.	B
2.	B	12.	B
3.	B	13.	C
4.	A	14.	D
5.	B	15.	C
6.	C	16.	C
7.	B	17.	A
8.	C	18.	A
9.	C	19.	D
10.	C	20.	D

TEST 2

DIRECTIONS: Each question or incomplete statement is followed by several suggested answers or completions. Select the one that BEST answers the question or completes the statement. *PRINT THE LETTER OF THE CORRECT ANSWER IN THE SPACE AT THE RIGHT.*

1. Assume that one of your subordinates, a supervisor in charge of a small unit in your bureau, asks your advice in handling a situation which has just occurred in his unit. On returning from a meeting, the supervisor notices that Jane Jones, the unit secretary, is not at her regular work location. Another employee had become faint, and the secretary accompanied this employee outdoors for some fresh air. It is a long-standing rule that no employee is permitted to leave the building during office hours except on official business or with the unit head's approval. Quite recently another employee was reprimanded by the supervisor for going out at 10 A.M. for a cup of coffee. 1.____
   Of the following, it would be BEST for you to advise the supervisor to
   A. circulate a memo within the unit, restating the department's regulation concerning leaving the building during office hours
   B. overlook this rule violation in view of the extenuating circumstances
   C. personally reprimand the unit secretary since all employees must be treated in the same way when official rules are broken
   D. tell the unit secretary that you should reprimand her, but that you've decided to overlook the rule infraction this time

2. Of the following, the MOST valid reason why the application of behavioral modification techniques to management of large organizations is not yet widely accepted by managers is these techniques are 2.____
   A. based mainly on research conducted under highly controlled conditions
   B. more readily adaptable to training unskilled employees
   C. incompatible with the validated *management-by-objectives* approach
   D. manipulative and incompatible with the democratic approach

3. Because of intensive pressures which have developed since the onset of the city's financial problems, the members of a certain bureau have begun to file grievances about their working conditions. These protests are accumulating at a much greater rate than normal and faster than they can be disposed of under the current state of affairs. Concerned about the possible effect of these unresolved matters on the productivity of the bureau at such a critical time, the administrator in charge decides to take immediate action to improve staff relations. 3.____
   With this intention in mind, he should
   A. explain to the staff why their grievances cannot be handled at the present time; then inform them that there will be a moratorium on the filing of additional grievances until the current backlog has been eliminated
   B. assemble all grievants at a special meeting and assure them that their problems will be handled in due course, but the current pressures preclude the prompt settling of their grievances

C. assign the assistant directors of the bureau to immediately schedule and conduct hearings on the accumulated grievances until the backlog is eliminated
D. suggest that the grievants again confer with their supervisors about their problems, orally rather than in writing, with direct appeal to him for such cases as are not resolved in this manner

4. A supervisor is attending a staff meeting with other accounting supervisors during which the participants are to propose various possible methods of dealing with a complex operational problem. 4.____
The one of the following procedures which will MOST likely produce an acceptable proposal for solving this problem at this meeting is for the
A. group to agree at the beginning of the meeting on the kinds of approaches to the problem that are most likely to succeed
B. conference leader to set a firm time limit on the period during which the participants are to present whatever ideas come to mind
C. group to discuss each proposal fully before the next proposal is made
D. conference leader to urge every participant in the meeting to present at least one proposal

5. Which one of the following types of communication systems would foster an authoritarian atmosphere in a large agency? 5.____
A communication system which
A. is restricted to organizational procedures and specific job instructions
B. provides information to employees about the rationale for their jobs
C. informs employees about their job performance
D. provides information about the relationship of employees' work to the agency's goals

6. According to most management experts, the one of the following which would generally have SERIOUS shortcomings as a component of a performance evaluation program is 6.____
A. rating the performance of each subordinate against the performance of other subordinates
B. limiting the appraisal to an evaluation of current performance
C. rating each subordinate in terms of clearly stated, measurable job goals
D. interviewing the subordinate to discuss present job performance and ways of improvement

7. Which of the following is consistent with the management-by-objectives approach as used in a fiscal affairs division of a large city agency? 7.____
A. Performance goals for the division are established by the administrator, who requires daily progress reports for each accounting unit.
B. Each subordinate accountant participates in setting his own short-term performance goals.
C. A detailed set of short-term performance goals for each accountant is prepared by his supervisor.
D. Objectives are established and progress evaluated by a committee of administrative accountants.

Questions 8-11.

DIRECTIONS: Questions 8 through 11 are to be answered on the basis of the following information.

Assume that you are the director of a small bureau, organized into three divisions. The bureau has a total of twenty employees: fourteen in professional titles and six in clerical titles. Each division has a chief who reports directly to you and who supervises five employees.

For Questions 8 through 11, you are to select the MOST appropriate training method, from the four choices given, based on the situation in the question:

A. Lecture, with a small blackboard available
B. Lecture, with audio-visual aids
C. Conference
D. Buddy system (experienced worker is accompanied by worker to be trained)

8. A major reorganization of your department was completed. You have decided to conduct a training session of about one hour's duration for all your subordinates in order to acquaint them with the new departmental structure as well as the new responsibilities which have been assigned to the divisions of your bureau. 8.____

9. Three assistant supervisors, each with one year of service in your department, are transferred to your bureau as part of the process of strengthening the major activity of your bureau. In connection with their duties, if they are required to do field visits to business firms located in the various industrial areas of the city. 9.____

10. The work of your bureau requires that various forms be processed sequentially through each of three divisions. In recent weeks, you have received complaints from the division chiefs that their production is being impeded by a lack of cooperation from the chiefs and workers in the other divisions. 10.____

11. In order to improve the efficiency of the department, your department head has directed that all bureaus hold weekly, thirty-minute-long training sessions for all employees, to review relevant work procedures. 11.____

12. Which one of the following actions is usually MOST appropriate for a manager to take in order to encourage and develop coordination of effort among different units or individuals within an organization? 12.____
    A. Providing rewards to the most productive employees
    B. Giving employees greater responsibility and the authority to exercise it
    C. Emphasizing to the employees that it is important to coordinate their efforts
    D. Explaining the goals of the organization to the employees and how their jobs relate to those goals

13. The management of time is one of the critical aspects of any supervisor's performance. 13.____
Therefore, in evaluating a subordinate from the viewpoint of how he manages time, a supervisor should rate HIGHEST the subordinate who
   A. concentrates on each task as he undertakes it
   B. performs at a standard and predictable pace under all circumstances
   C. takes shortened lunch periods when he is busy
   D. tries to do two things simultaneously

14. A MAJOR research finding regarding employee absenteeism is that 14.____
   A. absenteeism is likely to be higher on hot days
   B male employees tend to be absent more than female employees
   C. the way an employee is treated as a definite bearing on absenteeism
   D. the distance employees have to travel is one of the most important factors in absenteeism

15. Of the following, the supervisory behavior that is of GREATEST benefit to the organization is exhibited by supervisors who 15.____
   A. are strict with subordinates about following rules and regulations
   B. encourage subordinates to be interested in the work
   C. are willing to assist with subordinates' work on most occasions
   D. get the most done with available staff and resources

16. In order to maintain a proper relationship with a worker who is assigned to staff rather than line functions, a line supervisor should 16.____
   A. accept all recommendations of the staff worker
   B. include the staff worker in the conferences called by the supervisor for his subordinates
   C. keep the staff worker informed of developments in the area of his staff assignment
   D. require that the staff worker's recommendations be communicated to the supervisor through the supervisor's own superior

17. Of the following, the GREATEST disadvantage of placing a worker in a staff position under the direct supervision of the supervisor whom he advises is the possibility that the 17.____
   A. staff worker will tend to be insubordinate because of a feeling of superiority over the supervisor
   B. staff worker will tend to give advice of the type which the supervisor wants to hear or finds acceptable
   C. supervisor will tend to be mistrustful of the advice of a worker of subordinate rank
   D. supervisor will tend to derive little benefit from the advice because to supervise properly he should know at least as much as his subordinate

18. One factor which might be given consideration in deciding upon the optimum span of control of a supervisor over his immediate subordinates is the position of the supervisor in the hierarchy of the organization.
It is generally considered proper that the number of subordinates immediately supervised by a higher, upper echelon, supervisor 18.____
   A. is unrelated to and tends to form no pattern with the number of supervised by lower level supervisors
   B. should be about the same as the number supervised by a lower level supervisor
   C. should be larger than the number supervised by a lower level supervisor
   D. should be smaller than the number supervised by a lower level supervisor

19. Assume that you are a supervisor and have been assigned to assist the head of a large agency unit. He asks you to prepare a simple, functional organization chart of the unit.
Such a chart would be USEFUL for 19.____
   A. favorably impressing members of the public with the important nature of the agency's work
   B. graphically presenting staff relationships which may indicate previously unknown duplications, overlaps, and gaps in job duties
   C. motivating all employees toward better performance because they will have a better understanding of job procedures
   D. subtly and inoffensively making known to the staff in the unit that you are now in a position of responsibility

20. In some large organizations, management's traditional means of learning about employee dissatisfaction has been in the *open door policy.*
This policy USUALLY means that 20.____
   A. management lets it be known that a management representative is generally available to discuss employees' questions, suggestions, and complaints
   B. management sets up an informal employee organization to establish a democratic procedure for orderly representation of employees
   C. employees are encouraged to attempt to resolve dissatisfactions at the lowest possible level of authority
   D. employees are provided with an address or box so that they may safely and anonymously register complaints

KEY (CORRECT ANSWERS)

1.	B	11.	A
2.	A	12.	D
3.	D	13.	A
4.	B	14.	C
5.	A	15.	D
6.	A	16.	C
7.	B	17.	B
8.	B	18.	D
9.	D	19.	B
10.	C	20.	A

EXAMINATION SECTION

TEST 1

DIRECTIONS: Each question or incomplete statement is followed by several suggested answers or completions. Select the one that BEST answers the question or completes the statement. *PRINT THE LETTER OF THE CORRECT ANSWER IN THE SPACE AT THE RIGHT.*

1. It is often desirable for an administrator to consult, during the planning process, the persons to be affected by those plans. 1.____
Of the following, the MAJOR justification for such consultation is that it recognizes the
   A. fact that participating in horizontal planning is almost always more effective than participating in vertical planning
   B. principle of participation and the need for a sense of belonging as a means of decreasing resistance and developing support
   C. principle that lower-level administrators normally are more likely than higher-level administrators to emphasize longer-range goals
   D. fact that final responsibility for the approval of plans should be placed in committees not individuals

2. In evaluating performance and, if necessary, correcting what is being done to assure attainment of results according to plan, it is GENERALLY best for the administrator to do which one of the following? 2.____
   A. Make a continual effort to increase the number of written control reports prepared
   B. Thoroughly investigate in equal detail all possible deviations indicated by comparison of performance to expectation
   C. Decentralize, within an operating unit or division, the responsibility for correcting deviations
   D. Concentrate on the exceptions, or outstanding variations, from the expected results or standards

3. Generally, changes in the ways in which the supervisors and employees in an organization do things are MORE likely to be welcomed by them when the changes 3.____
   A. threaten the security of the supervisors than when they do not
   B. are inaugurated after prior change has been assimilated than when they are inaugurated before other major changes have been assimilated
   C. follow a series of failures in changes when they follow a series of successful changes
   D. are dictated by personal order rather than when they result from an application of previously established impersonal principles

4. For sound organization relationships, of the following, it is generally MOST desirable that 4.____
   A. authority and responsibility be segregated from each other, in order to facilitate control
   B. the authority of a manager should be commensurate with his responsibility, and vice versa
   C. authority be defined as the obligation of an individual to carry out assigned activities to the best of his or her ability
   D. clear recognition be given to the fact that delegation of authority benefits only the manager who delegates it

5. In utilizing a checklist of questions for general managerial planning, which one of the following generally is the FIRST question to be asked and answered? 5.____
   A. Where will it take place?
   B. How will it be done?
   C. Why must it be done?
   D. Who will do it?

6. Of the following, it is USUALLY best to set administrative objectives so that they are 6.____
   A. at a level that is unattainable, so that administrators will continually be strongly motivated
   B. at a level that is attainable, but requires some stretching and reaching by administrators trying to attain them
   C. stated in qualitative rather than quantitative terms whenever a choice between the two is possible
   D. stated in a general and unstructured manner, to permit each administrator maximum freedom in interpreting them

7. In selecting from among administrative alternatives, three general bases for decisions are open to the manager – experience, experimentation, and research and analysis. Of the following, the best argument AGAINST primary reliance upon experimentation as the method of evaluating administrative alternatives is that experimentation is 7.____
   A. generally the most expensive of the three techniques
   B. almost always legally prohibited in procedural matters
   C. possible only in areas where results may be easily duplicated by other experimenters at any time
   D. an approach that requires information on scientific method seldom available to administrators

8. The administrator who utilizes the techniques of operations research, linear programming and simulation in making an administrative decision should MOST appropriately be considered to be using the techniques of ______ analysis. 8.____
   A. intuitive B. quantitative
   C. nonmathematical D. qualitative

9. When an additional organizational level is added within a department, that department has MOST directly manifested 9.____
   A. horizontal growth B. horizontal shrinkage
   C. vertical growth D. vertical shrinkage

10. Of the following, the one which GENERALLY is the most intangible planning factor is 10.____
    A. budget dollars allocated to a function
    B. square feet of space for office use
    C. number of personnel in various clerical titles
    D. emotional impact of a proposed personnel policy among employees

11. Departmentation by function is the same as, or most similar to, departmentation by 11.____
    A. equipment B. clientele
    C. territory D. activity

12. Such verifiable factors as turnover, absenteeism or volume of grievances would generally BEST assist in measuring the effectiveness of a program to improve 12.____
    A. forms control B. employee morale
    C. linear programming D. executive creativity

13. An organization increases the number of subordinates reporting to a manager up to the point where incremental savings in costs, better communication and morale, and other factors equal incremental losses in effectiveness of control, direction and similar factors. This action MOST specifically employs the technique of 13.____
    A. role playing
    B. queuing theory
    C. marginal analysis
    D. capital standards analysis

14. The term *computer hardware* is MOST likely to refer to 14.____
    A. machines and equipment
    B. Ethernet and USB cables
    C. training manuals
    D. word processing and spreadsheet programs

15. Determining what is being accomplished, that is, evaluating the performance and, if necessary, applying corrective measures so that performance takes place according to plans is MOST appropriately called management 15.____
    A. actuating B. planning
    C. controlling D. motivating

16. Of the following, the BEST overall technique for choosing from among several alternative public programs proposed to try to achieve the same broad objective generally is ______ analysis. 16.____
   A. random-sample
   B. input
   C. cost-effectiveness
   D. output

17. When the success of a plan in achieving specific program objectives is measured against that plan's costs, the measure obtained is most directly that of the plan's 17.____
   A. pervasiveness
   B. control potential
   C. primacy
   D. efficiency

18. Generally, the degree to which an organization's planning will be coordinated varies MOST directly with the degree to which 18.____
   A. the individuals charged with executing plans are better compensated than those charged with developing and evaluating plans
   B. the individuals charged with planning understand and agree to utilize consistent planning premises
   C. a large number of position classification titles have been established for those individuals charged with organizational planning functions
   D. subordinate unit objectives are allowed to control the overall objectives of the departments of which such subordinate units are a part

19. The responsibility for specific types of decisions generally is BEST delegated to 19.____
   A. the highest organizational level at which there is an individual possessing the ability, desire, impartiality and access to relevant information needed to make these decisions
   B. the lowest organizational level at which there is an individual possessing the ability, desire, impartiality and access to relevant information needed to make these decisions
   C. a group of executives, rather than a single executive, if these decisions deal with an emergency
   D. the organizational level midway between that which will have to carry out these decisions and that which will have to authorize the resources for their implementation

20. The process of managing by objectives is MOST likely to lead to a situation in which the 20.____
   A. goal accomplishment objectives of managers tend to have a longer timespan as one goes lower down the line in an organization
   B. establishment of quantitative goals for staff positions is generally easier than the establishment of quantitative goals for line positions
   C. development of objectives requires the manager to think of the way he will accomplish given results, and of the organization, personnel and resources that he will need
   D. superiors normally develop and finally approve detailed goals for subordinates without any prior consultation with either those subordinates or with the top-level executives responsible for the longer-run objectives of the organization

21. As used with respect to decision making, the application of scientific method to the study of alternatives in a problem situation, with a view to providing a quantitative basis for arriving at an optimum solution in terms of the goals sought is MOST appropriately called 21.____
   A. simple number departmentation
   B. geographic decentralization
   C. operations research
   D. trait rating

22. Assume that a bureau head proposes that final responsibility and authority for all planning within the bureau is to be delegated to one employee who is to be paid at the level of an assistant division head in that bureau. 22.____
Of the following, the MOST appropriate comment about this proposal is that it's
   A. *improper*, mainly because planning does not call for someone at such a high level
   B. *improper*, mainly because responsibility for a basic management function such as planning may not properly be delegated as proposed
   C. *proper*, mainly because ultimate responsibility for all bureau planning is best placed as proposed
   D. *proper*, mainly because every well-managed bureau should have a full-time planning officer

23. Of the following, the MOST important reason that participation has motivating effects is generally that it gives to the individual participating 23.____
   A. a recognition of his or her desire to feel important and to contribute to achievement of worthwhile goals
   B. an opportunity to participate in work that is beyond the scope of the class specification for his or her title
   C. a secure knowledge that his or her organization's top leadership is as efficient as possible considering all major circumstances
   D. the additional information likely to be crucial to his or her promotion

24. Of the following, the MOST essential characteristic of an effective employee suggestion system is that 24.____
   A. suggestions be submitted upward through the chain of command
   B. suggestions be acted upon promptly so that employees may be promptly informed of what happens to their submitted suggestions
   C. suggesters be required to sign their names on the material sent to the actual evaluators for evaluation
   D. suggesters receive at least 25% of the agency's savings during the first two years after their suggestions have been accepted and put into effect by the agency

25. Two organizations have the same basic objectives and the same total number of employees. The span of authority of each intermediate manager is narrower in one organization than it is in the other. It is MOST likely that the organization in which each intermediate manager has a narrower span of authority will have 25.____
    A. fewer intermediate managers
    B. more organizational levels
    C. more managers reporting to a larger number of intermediate supervisors
    D. more characteristics of a *flat* organizational structure

KEY (CORRECT ANSWERS)

1.	B	11.	D
2.	D	12.	B
3.	B	13.	C
4.	B	14.	A
5.	C	15.	C
6.	B	16.	C
7.	A	17.	D
8.	B	18.	B
9.	C	19.	B
10.	D	20.	C

21. C
22. B
23. A
24. B
25. B

TEST 2

DIRECTIONS: Each question or incomplete statement is followed by several suggested answers or completions. Select the one that BEST answers the question or completes the statement. *PRINT THE LETTER OF THE CORRECT ANSWER IN THE SPACE AT THE RIGHT.*

1. Which one of the following BEST expresses the essence of the merit idea or system in public employment? 1.____
   A. A person's worth to the organization—the merit of his or her attributes and capacities—is the governing factor in his or her selection, assignment, pay, recognition, advancement and retention
   B. Written tests of the objective type are the only fair way to select on a merit basis from among candidates for open-competitive appointment to positions within the merit system
   C. Employees who have qualified for civil service positions shall have lifetime tenure during good behavior in those positions regardless of changes in public programs
   D. Periodic examinations with set date limits within which all persons desiring to demonstrate their merit may apply, shall be publicly advertised and held for all promotional titles

2. Of the following, the promotion selection policy generally considered MOST antithetical to the merit concept is the promotion selection policy which 2.____
   A. is based solely on objective tests of competence
   B. is based solely on seniority
   C. may require a manager to lose his or her best employee to another part of the organization
   D. permits operating managers collectively to play a significant role in promotion decisions

3. Of the following, the problems encountered by government establishments which are MOST likely to make extensive delegation of authority difficult to effectuate tend to be problems of 3.____
   A. accountability and ensuring uniform administration
   B. line and staff relationships within field offices
   C. generally employee opposition to such delegation of authority and to the subsequent record-keeping activities
   D. use of the management-by-objectives approach

4. The major decisions as to which jobs shall be created and who shall carry which responsibilities should GENERALLY be made by 4.____
   A. budgetary advisers
   B. line managers
   C. classification specialists
   D. peer-level rating committees

5. The ultimate controlling factor in structuring positions in the public service, MOST generally, should be the 5.____
   A. possibility of providing upgrading for highly productive employees
   B. collective bargaining demands initially made by established public employee unions
   C. positive motivational effects upon productivity resulting from an inverted pyramid job structure
   D. effectiveness of the structuring in serving the mission of the organization

6. Of the following, the most usual reason for unsatisfactory line-staff relationships is 6.____
   A. inept use of the abilities of staff personnel by line management
   B. the higher salaries paid to line officials
   C. excessive consultation between line officials and staff officials at the same organizational level
   D. a feeling among the staff members that only lower-level line members appreciate their work

7. Generally, an employee receiving new information from a fellow employee is MOST likely to 7.____
   A. forget the new information if it is consistent with his or her existing beliefs much more easily than he or she forgets the new information if it is inconsistent with existing beliefs
   B. accept the validity of the new information if it is consistent with his or her existing beliefs more readily than he or she accepts the validity of the new information if it is inconsistent with existing beliefs
   C. have a less accurate memory of the new information if it is consistent with his or her existing beliefs than he or she has of the new information if it is inconsistent with existing beliefs
   D. ignore the new information if it is consistent with his or her existing beliefs more often than he or she ignores the new information if it is inconsistent with existing beliefs

8. Virtually all of us use this principle in our human communications – perhaps without realizing it. In casual conversations, we are alert for cues to whether we are understood (e.g., attentive nods from the other person). Similarly, an instructor is always interested in reactions among those to whom he is giving instruction. The effective administrator is equally conscious of the need to determine his or her subordinates' reactions to what he or she is trying to communicate. 8.____
   The principle referred to in the above selection is MOST appropriately called
   A. cognitive dissonance B. feedback
   C. negative reinforcement D. noise transmission

9. Of the following, the PRINCIPAL function of an *ombudsman* generally is to 9.____
   A. review departmental requests for new data processing equipment so as to reduce duplication
   B. receive and investigate complaints from citizens who are displeased with the actions or non-actions of administrative officials and try to effectuate warranted remedies
   C. review proposed departmental reorganizations in order to advise the chief executive whether or not they are in accordance with the latest principles of proper management structuring
   D. presiding over courts of the judiciary convened to try *sitting* judges

10. Of the following, the MOST valid reason for recruiting an intermediate-level administrator from outside an agency, rather than from within the agency, normally is to 10.____
    A. improve the public image of the agency as a desirable place in which to be employed
    B. reduce the number of potential administrators who must be evaluated prior to filling the position
    C. minimize the morale problems arising from frequent internal staff upgradings
    D. obtain fresh ideas and a fresh viewpoint on agency problems

11. A MAJOR research finding regarding employee absenteeism is that 11.____
    A. absenteeism is likely to be higher on hot days
    B male employees tend to be absent more than female employees
    C. the way an employee is treated as a definite bearing on absenteeism
    D. the distance employees have to travel is one of the most important factors in absenteeism

12. Of the following, the supervisory behavior that is of GREATEST benefit to the organization is exhibited by supervisors who 12.____
    A. are strict with subordinates about following rules and regulations
    B. encourage subordinates to be interested in the work
    C. are willing to assist with subordinates' work on most occasions
    D. get the most done with available staff and resources

13. The management of time is one of the critical aspects of any supervisor's performance. 13.____
Therefore, in evaluating a subordinate from the viewpoint of how he manages time, a supervisor should rate HIGHEST the subordinate who
   A. concentrates on each task as he undertakes it
   B. performs at a standard and predictable pace under all circumstances
   C. takes shortened lunch periods when he is busy
   D. tries to do two things simultaneously

14. A MAJOR research finding regarding employee absenteeism is that 14.____
   A. absenteeism is likely to be higher on hot days
   B male employees tend to be absent more than female employees
   C. the way an employee is treated as a definite bearing on absenteeism
   D. the distance employees have to travel is one of the most important factors in absenteeism

15. Of the following, the supervisory behavior that is of GREATEST benefit to the organization is exhibited by supervisors who 15.____
   A. are strict with subordinates about following rules and regulations
   B. encourage subordinates to be interested in the work
   C. are willing to assist with subordinates' work on most occasions
   D. get the most done with available staff and resources

16. In order to maintain a proper relationship with a worker who is assigned to staff rather than line functions, a line supervisor should 16.____
   A. accept all recommendations of the staff worker
   B. include the staff worker in the conferences called by the supervisor for his subordinates
   C. keep the staff worker informed of developments in the area of his staff assignment
   D. require that the staff worker's recommendations be communicated to the supervisor through the supervisor's own superior

17. Of the following, the GREATEST disadvantage of placing a worker in a staff position under the direct supervision of the supervisor whom he advises is the possibility that the 17.____
   A. staff worker will tend to be insubordinate because of a feeling of superiority over the supervisor
   B. staff worker will tend to give advice of the type which the supervisor wants to hear or finds acceptable
   C. supervisor will tend to be mistrustful of the advice of a worker of subordinate rank
   D. supervisor will tend to derive little benefit from the advice because to supervise properly he should know at least as much as his subordinate

18. One factor which might be given consideration in deciding upon the optimum span of control of a supervisor over his immediate subordinates is the position of the supervisor in the hierarchy of the organization. 18.____
It is generally considered proper that the number of subordinates immediately supervised by a higher, upper echelon, supervisor
    A. is unrelated to and tends to form no pattern with the number of supervised by lower level supervisors
    B. should be about the same as the number supervised by a lower level supervisor
    C. should be larger than the number supervised by a lower level supervisor
    D. should be smaller than the number supervised by a lower level supervisor

19. Assume that you are a supervisor and have been assigned to assist the head of a large agency unit. He asks you to prepare a simple, functional organization chart of the unit. 19.____
Such a chart would be USEFUL for
    A. favorably impressing members of the public with the important nature of the agency's work
    B. graphically presenting staff relationships which may indicate previously unknown duplications, overlaps, and gaps in job duties
    C. motivating all employees toward better performance because they will have a better understanding of job procedures
    D. subtly and inoffensively making known to the staff in the unit that you are now in a position of responsibility

20. In some large organizations, management's traditional means of learning about employee dissatisfaction has been in the *open door policy*. 20.____
This policy USUALLY means that
    A. management lets it be known that a management representative is generally available to discuss employees' questions, suggestions, and complaints
    B. management sets up an informal employee organization to establish a democratic procedure for orderly representation of employees
    C. employees are encouraged to attempt to resolve dissatisfactions at the lowest possible level of authority
    D. employees are provided with an address or box so that they may safely and anonymously register complaints

KEY (CORRECT ANSWERS)

1.	B	11.	A
2.	A	12.	D
3.	D	13.	A
4.	B	14.	C
5.	A	15.	D
6.	A	16.	C
7.	B	17.	B
8.	B	18.	D
9.	D	19.	B
10.	C	20.	A

EXAMINATION SECTION

TEST 1

DIRECTIONS: Each question or incomplete statement is followed by several suggested answers or completions. Select the one that BEST answers the question or completes the statement. *PRINT THE LETTER OF THE CORRECT ANSWER IN THE SPACE AT THE RIGHT.*

1. An executive assigns A, the head of a staff unit, to devise plans for reducing the delay in submittal of reports by a local agency headed by C. The reports are under the supervision of C's subordinate line official B with whom A is to deal directly. In his investigation, A finds: (1) the reasons for the delay; and (2) poor practices which have either been overlooked or condoned by line official B. 1.____
Of the following courses of action A could take, the BEST one would be to
   A. develop recommendations with line official B with regard to reducing the delay and correcting the poor practice and then report fully to his own executive
   B. discuss the findings with C in an attempt to correct the situation before making any formal report on the poor practices
   C. report both findings to his executive, attaching the explanation offered by C
   D. report to his executive on the first finding and discuss the second in a friendly way with line official B
   E. report the first finding to his executive, ignoring the second until his opinion is requested

2. Drafts of a proposed policy, prepared by a staff committee, are circulated to ten member of the field staff of the organization by route slips with a request for comments within two weeks. Two members of the field staff make extensive comments, four offer editorial suggestions, and the remainder make minor favorable comments. Shortly after, it found that the statement needs considerable revision by the field staff. 2.____
Of the following possible reasons for the original failure of the field staff to identify difficulties, the MOST likely is that the
   A. field staff did not take sufficient time to review the manual
   B. field staff had not been advised of the type of contribution expected
   C. low morale of the field staff prevented their showing interest
   D. policy statement was too advanced for the staff
   E. staff committee was not sufficiently representative

3. Operator participation in management improvement work is LEAST likely to 3.____
   A. assure the use of best available management technique
   B. overcome the stigma of the outside expert
   C. place responsibility for improvement in the person who knows the job best
   D. simplify installation
   E. take advantage of the desire of most operators to seek self-improvement

4. In general, the morale of workers in an agency is MOST frequently and MOST significantly affected by the 4.____
   A. agency policies of organizational structure and operational procedures
   B. distance of the employee's job from his home community
   C. fringe benefits
   D. number of opportunities for advancement
   E. relationship with supervisors

5. Of the following, the PRIMARY function of a work distribution chart is to 5.____
   A. analyze the soundness of existing divisions of labor
   B. eliminate the unnecessary clerical detail
   C. establish better supervisory techniques
   D. simplify work methods
   E. weed out core functions

6. In analyzing a process chart, which one of the following should be asked FIRST? 6.____
   A. How B. When C. Where D. Who E. Why

7. Which one of the following is NOT an advantage of the interview method of collecting data? It 7.____
   A. enables interviewer to judge the person interviewed on such matters as general attitude, knowledge, etc.
   B. helps build up personal relations for later installation of changes
   C. is a flexible method that can be adjusted to changing circumstances
   D. permits the obtaining of *off the record* information
   E. produces more accurate information than other methods

8. Which one of the following may be defined as a *regularly recurring appraisal of the manner in which all elements of agency management are being carried out*? 8.____
   A. Functional survey B. Operations audit
   C. Organization survey D. Over-all survey
   E. Reconnaissance survey

9. An analysis of the flow of work in a department should begin with the _____ work. 9.____
   A. major routine B. minor routine C. supervisory
   D. technical E. unusual

10. Which method would MOST likely be used to get first-hand information on complaints from the public? 10.____
   A. Study of correspondence
   B. Study of work volume
   C. Tracing specific transactions through a series of steps
   D. Tracing use of forms
   E. Worker desk audit

11. People will generally produce the MOST if 11.____
    A. management exercises close supervision over the work
    B. there is strict discipline in the group
    C. they are happy in their work
    D. they feel involved in their work
    E. they follow *the one best way*

12. The normal analysis of which chart listed below is MOST closely related to organizational analysis? ______ chart. 12.____
    A. Layout B. Operation C. Process
    D. Work count E. Work distribution

13. The work count would be LEAST helpful in accomplishing which one of the following? 13.____
    A. Demonstrating personnel needs B. Improving the sequence of steps
    C. Measuring the value of a step D. Spotting bottlenecks
    E. Stimulating interest in work

14. Which one of the following seems LEAST useful as a guide in interviewing an employee in a procedure and methods survey? 14.____
    A. Explaining who you are and the purpose of your visit
    B. Having a general plan of what you intend to get from the interview
    C. Listening carefully and not interrupting
    D. Trying out his reactions to your ideas for improvements
    E. Trying to analyze his reasons for saying what he says

15. Which one of the following is an advantage of the questionnaire method of gathering facts as compared with the interview method? 15.____
    A. Different people may interpret the questions differently
    B. Less *off the record* information is given
    C. More time may be taken in order to give exact answers
    D. Personal relationships with the people involved are not established
    E. There is less need for follow-up

16. Which one of the following is generally NOT an advantage of the personal observation method of gathering facts? It 16.____
    A. enables staff to use *off the record* information if personally observed
    B. helps in developing valid recommendations
    C. helps the person making the observation acquire *know how* valuable for later installation and follow-up
    D. is economical in time and money
    E. may turn up other problems in need of solution

17. Which of the following would MOST often be the best way to minimize resistance to change? 17.____
    A. Break the news about the change gently to the people affected
    B. Increase the salary of the people affected by the change
    C. Let the people concerned participate at the decision to change

D. Notify all people concerned with the change, both orally and in writing
E. Stress the advantages of the new system

18. The functional organization chart 18.____
A. does not require periodic revision
B. includes a description of the duties of each organization segment
C. includes positions and titles for each organization segment
D. is the simplest type of organization chart
E. is used primarily by newly established agencies

19. The principle of span of control has frequently been said to be in conflict with the 19.____
A. principle of unity of command
B. principle that authority should be commensurate with responsibility
C. principle that like functions should be grouped into one unit
D. principle that the number of levels between the top of an organization and the bottom should be small
E. scalar principle

20. If an executive delegates to his subordinates authority to handle problems of a routine nature for which standard solutions have been established, he may expect that 20.____
A. fewer complaint will be received
B. he has made it more difficult for his subordinates to solve these problems
C. he has opened the way for confusion in his organization
D. there will be a lack of consistency in the methods applied to the solution of these problems
E. these routine problems will be handled efficiently and he will have more time for other non-routine work

21. Which of the following would MOST likely be achieved by a change in the basic organization structure from the *process* or *functional* type to the *purpose* or *product* type? 21.____
A. Easier recruitment of personnel in a tight labor market
B. Fixing responsibility at a lower level in the organization
C. Greater centralization
D. Greater economy
E. Greater professional development

22. Usually the MOST difficult problem in connection with a major reorganization is 22.____
A. adopting a pay plan to fit the new structure
B. bringing the organization manual up-to-date
C. determining the new organization structure
D. gaining acceptance of the new plan by the higher level employees
E. gaining acceptance of the new plan by the lower level employees

23. Which of the following statements MOST accurately describes the work of the chiefs of MOST staff divisions in departments? 23.____
Chiefs
   A. focus more on getting the job done than on how it is done
   B. are mostly interested in short-range results
   C. nearly always advise but rarely advise
   D. usually command or control but rarely advise
   E. provide service to the rest of the organization and/or assist the chief executive in planning and controlling operations

24. In determining the type of organization structure of an enterprise, the one factor that might be given relatively greater weight in a small organization than in a larger organization of the same nature is the 24.____
   A. geographical location of the enterprise
   B. individual capabilities of incumbents
   C. method of financing to be employed
   D. size of the area served
   E. type of activity engaged in

25. Functional foremanship differs MOST markedly from generally accepted principle of administration in that it advocates 25.____
   A. an unlimited span of control
   B. less delegation of responsibility
   C. more than one supervisor for an employee
   D. nonfunctional organization
   E. substitution of execution for planning

KEY (CORRECT ANSWERS)

1.	A	11.	D
2.	B	12.	E
3.	A	13.	B
4.	E	14.	D
5.	A	15.	C
6.	E	16.	D
7.	E	17.	C
8.	B	18.	B
9.	A	19.	D
10.	A	20.	E

21.	B
22.	D
23.	E
24.	B
25.	C

TEST 2

DIRECTIONS: Each question or incomplete statement is followed by several suggested answers or completions. Select the one that BEST answers the question or completes the statement. *PRINT THE LETTER OF THE CORRECT ANSWER IN THE SPACE AT THE RIGHT.*

1. Decentralization of the authority to make decisions is a necessary result of increased complexity in an organization, but for the sake of efficiency and coordination of operations, such decentralization must be planned carefully. A good general rule is that 1.____
   A. any decision should be made at the lowest possible point in the organization where all the information and competence necessary for a sound decision are available
   B. any decision should be made at the highest possible point in the organization, thus guaranteeing the best decision
   C. any decision should be made at the lowest possible point in the organization, but always approved by management
   D. any decision should be made by management and referred to the proper subordinate for comment
   E. no decision should be made by any individual in the organization without approval by a superior

2. One drawback of converting a conventional consecutive filing system to a terminal digit filing system for a large installation is that 2.____
   A. conversion would be expensive in time and manpower
   B. conversion would prevent the proper use of recognized numeric classification systems, such as the Dewey decimal, in classifying files material
   C. responsibility for proper filing cannot be pinpointed in the terminal digit system
   D. the terminal digit system requires considerably more space than a normal filing system

3. The basic filing system that would ordinarily be employed in a large administrative headquarters unit is the _____ file system. 3.____
   A alphabetic
   B. chronological
   C. mnemonic
   D. retention
   E. subject classification

4. A records center is of benefit in a records management program PRIMARILY because 4.____
   A. all the records of the organization are kept in one place
   B. inactive records can be stored economically in less expense storage areas
   C. it provides a place where useless records can be housed at little or no cost to the organization

D. obsolete filing and storage equipment can be utilized out of view of the public
E. records analysts can examine an organization's files without affecting the unit's operation or upsetting the supervisors

5. In examining a number of different forms to see whether any could be combined or eliminated, which of the following would one be MOST likely to use? 5.____
A. Forms analysis sheet of recurring data
B. Forms control log
C. Forms design and approval request
D. Forms design and guide sheet
E. Numerical file

6. The MOST important reason for control of *bootleg* forms is that 6.____
A. they are more expensive than authorized forms
B. they are usually poorly designed
C. they can lead to unnecessary procedures
D. they cannot be reordered as easily as authorized terms
E. violation of rules and regulations should not be allowed

7. With a box design of a form, the caption title or question to be answered should be located in the _____ of the box. 7.____
A. center at the bottom
B. center at the top
C. lower left corner
D. lower right corner
E. upper left corner

8. A two-part snapout form would be MOST properly justified if 8.____
A. it is a cleaner operation
B. it is prepared ten times a week
C. it saves time in preparation
D. it is to be filled out by hand rather than by typewriter
E. proper registration is critical

9. When deciding whether or not to approve a request for a new form, which reference is normally MOST pertinent? 9.____
A. Alphabetical Forms File
B. Functional Forms File
C. Numerical Forms File
D. Project Completion Report
E. Records Retention Data

10. Which of the following statements BEST explains the significance of the famed Hawthorne Plant experiments? 10.____
They showed that
A. a large span of control leads to more production than a small span of control
B. morale has no relationship to production
C. personnel counseling is of relatively little importance in a going organization

D. the special attention received by a group in an experimental situation has a greater impact on production than changes in working conditions
E. there is a direct relationship between the amount of illumination and production

11. Which of the following would most often NOT result from a highly efficient management control system? 11.____
A. Facilitation of delegation
B. Highlighting of problem areas
C. Increase in willingness of people to experiment or to take calculated risks
D. Provision of an objective test of new ideas or new methods and procedures
E. Provision of information useful for revising objectives, programs, and operations

12. The PERT system is a 12.____
A. method for laying out office space on a modular basis utilizing prefabricated partitions
B. method of motivating personnel to be continuously alert and to improve their appearance
C. method of program planning and control using a network or flow plan
D. plan for expanding reporting techniques
E. simplified method of cost accounting

13. The term *management control* is MOST frequently used to mean 13.____
A. an objective and unemotional approach by management
B. coordinating the efforts of all parts of the organization
C. evaluation of results in relation to plan
D. giving clear, precise orders to subordinates
E. keeping unions from making managerial decisions

14. Which one of the following factors has the MOST bearing on the frequency with which a control report should be made? 14.____
A. Degree of specialization of the work
B. Degree of variability in activities
C. Expense of the report
D. Number of levels of supervision
E. Number of personnel involved

15. The value of statistical records is MAINLY dependent upon the 15.____
A. method of presenting the material
B. number of items used
C. range of cases sampled
D. reliability of the information used
E. time devoted to compiling the material

16. When a supervisor delegates an assignment, he should 16.____
   A. delegate his responsibility for the assignment
   B. make certain that the assignment is properly performed
   C. participate in the beginning and final stages of the assignment
   D. retail all authority needed to complete the assignment
   E oversee all stages of the assignment

17. Assume that the department in which you are employed has never given official sanction to a mid-afternoon coffee break. Some bureaus have it and others do not. In the latter case, some individuals merely absent themselves for about 15 minutes at 3 P.M. while others remain on the job despite the fatigue which seems to be common among all employees in this department at that time. 17.____
   The course of action which you should recommend, if possible, is to
   A. arrange a schedule of mid-afternoon coffee breaks for all employees
   B. forbid all employees to take a mid-afternoon coffee break
   C. permit each bureau to decide for itself whether or not it will have a coffee break
   D. require all employees who wish a coffee break to take a shorter lunch period
   E. arrange a poll to discover the consensus of the department

18. The one of the following which is LEAST important in the management of a suggestion program is 18.____
   A. giving awards which are of sufficient value to encourage competition
   B. securing full support from the department's officers and executives
   C. publicizing the program and the awards given
   D. holding special conferences to analyze and evaluate some of the suggestions needed
   E. providing suggestion boxes in numerous locations

19. The one of the following which is MOST likely to decrease morale is 19.____
   A. insistence on strict adherence to safety rules
   B. making each employee responsible for the tidiness of his work area
   C. overlooking evidence of hostility between groups of employees
   D. strong, aggressive leadership
   E. allocating work on the basis of personal knowledge of the abilities and interests of the member of the department

20. Assume that a certain office procedure has been standard practice for many years. 20.____
   When a new employee asks why this particular procedure is followed, the supervisor should FIRST
   A. explain that everyone does it that way
   B. explain the reason for the procedure
   C. inform him that it has always been done that way in that particular office
   D. tell him to try it for a while before asking questions
   E. tell him he has never thought about it that way

21. Several employees complain informally to their supervisor regarding some new procedures which have been instituted. 21.____
The supervisor should IMMEDIATELY
A. explain that management is responsible
B. state frankly that he had nothing to do with it
C. refer the matter to the methods analyst
D. tell the employees to submit their complaint as a formal grievance
E. investigate the complaint

22. A new employee asks his supervisor how he is doing. Actually, he is not doing well in some phases of the job, but it is felt that he will learn in time. 22.____
The BEST response for the supervisor to make is:
A. Some things you are doing well, and in others I am sure you will improve.
B. Wait until the end of your probation period when we will discuss this matter.
C. You are not doing too well.
D. You are doing very well.
E. I'll be able to tell you when I go over your record.

23. The PRINCIPAL aim of a supervisor is to 23.____
A. act as liaison between employee and management
B. get the work done
C. keep up morale
D. train his subordinates
E. become chief of the department

24. When the work of two bureaus must be coordinated, direct contact between the subordinates in each bureau who are working on the problem is 24.____
A. *bad*, because it violates the chain of command
B. *bad*, because they do not have authority to make decisions
C. *good*, because it enable quicker results
D. *good*, because it relieves their superiors of any responsibilities
E. *bad*, because they may work at cross purposes

25. Of the following, the organization defect which can be ascertained MOST readily merely by analyzing an accurate and well-drawn organization chart is 25.____
A. ineffectiveness of an activity
B. improper span of control
C. inappropriate assignment of functions
D. poor supervision
E. unlawful delegation of authority

KEY (CORRECT ANSWERS)

1.	A	11.	C
2.	A	12.	C
3.	E	13.	C
4.	B	14.	B
5.	A	15.	D
6.	C	16.	B
7.	E	17.	A
8.	E	18.	E
9.	B	19.	C
10.	D	20.	B

21.	E
22.	A
23.	B
24.	C
25.	B

EXAMINATION SECTION
TEST 1

DIRECTIONS: Each question or incomplete statement is followed by several suggested answers or completions. Select the one that BEST answers the question or completes the statement. *PRINT THE LETTER OF THE CORRECT ANSWER IN THE SPACE AT THE RIGHT.*

1. An administrator in a department should be thoroughly familiar with modern methods of personnel administration. This statement is 1.____

    A. true, because this familiarity will help him in performing the normal functions of his office
    B. false, because personnel administration is not a departmental matter, but is centralized in the Civil Service Commission
    C. *true,* because this knowledge will insure the elimination of personnel problems in the department
    D. *false,* because departmental problems of a minor character are handled by the personnel representative, while major problems are the responsibility of the commissioner

2. The LEAST true of the following is that an administrative assistant in a department 2.____

    A. executes the policy laid down by the commissioner or his deputies
    B. in the main, carries out the policies of the commissioner but with some leeway where his own frame of reference is determinative
    C. is never required to formulate policy
    D. is responsible for the successful accomplishment of a section of the department's program

3. If a representative committee of employees in a large department is to meet with an administrative officer for the purpose of improving staff relations and of handling grievances, it is BEST that these meetings be held 3.____

    A. at regular intervals
    B. whenever requested by an aggrieved employee
    C. at the discretion of the administrative officer
    D. whenever the need arises

4. In the theory and practice of public administration, the one of the following which is LEAST generally regarded as a staff function is 4.____

    A. budgeting
    B. fire fighting
    C. purchasing
    D. research and information

5. The LEAST essential factor in the successful application of a service rating system is 5.____

    A. careful training of reporting officers
    B. provision for self–rating
    C. statistical analysis to check reliability
    D. utilization of objective standards of performance

6. Of the following, the one which is NOT an aim of service rating plans is 6._____

A. establishment of a fair method of measuring employee value to the employer
B. application of a uniform measurement to employees of the same class and grade performing similar functions
C. application of a uniform measurement to employees of the same class and grade however different their assignments may be
D. establishment of a scientific duties plan

7. A rule or regulation relating to the internal management of a department becomes effective 7._____

A. only after it is filed in the office of the clerk
B. as soon as issued by the department head
C. only after it has been published officially
D. when approved by the mayor

8. Of the following, the one MOST generally regarded as an *administrative* power is the 8._____

A. veto power
B. message power
C. power of pardon
D. rule making power

9. In public administration functional allocation involves 9._____

A. integration and the assignment of administrative power
B. the assignment of a single power to a single administrative level
C. the distribution of a number of subsidiary responsibilities among all levels of government
D. decentralization of administrative responsibilities

10. In the field of public administration, the LEAST general result of coordination is the 10._____

A. performance of a well–rounded job
B. elimination of jurisdictional overlapping
C. performance of functions otherwise neglected
D. elimination of duplication of work

11. Of the following, the MOST complicated and difficult problem confronting the reorganizer in the field of public administration is 11._____

A. ridding the government of graft
B. ridding the government of crude incompetence
C. ridding the government of excessive decentralization
D. conditioning organization to modern social and economic life

12. The *most accurate* description of the process of integration in the field of public administration is 12._____

A. transfer of administrative authority from a lower to a higher level of government
B. transfer of administrative authority from a higher to a lower level of government
C. concentration of administrative authority within one level of government
D. formal cooperation between city and state governments to administer a function

13. The one of the following who was *most closely* allied with *scientific management* is 13.____

A. Mosher B. Probst C. Taylor D. White

14. Of the following wall colors, the one which will reflect the GREATEST amount of light, other things being equal, is 14.____

A. buff B. light gray C. light blue D. brown

15. Natural illumination is LEAST necessary in a(n) 15.____

A. executive office
B. reception room
C. central stenographic bureau
D. conference room

16. The MOST desirable relative humidity in an office is 16.____

A. 30% B. 50% C. 70% D. 90%

17. When several pieces of correspondence are filed in the same folder they are *usually* arranged 17.____

A. according to subject
B. numerically
C. in the order in which they are received
D. alphabetically

18. Eliminating slack in work assignments is 18.____

A. speed-up
B. time study
C. motion study
D. efficient managment

19. *Time studies* examine and measure 19.____

A. past performance
B. present performance
C. long-run effect
D. influence of change

20. In making a position analysis for a duties classification, the one of the following factors which must be considered is the 20.____

A. capabilities of the incumbent
B. qualifications of the incumbent
C. efficiency attained by the incumbent
D. responsibility assigned to the incumbent

21. The MAXIMUM number of subordinates who can be effectively supervised by one administrative assistant is BEST considered as 21.____

A. determined by the law of *span of control*
B. determined by the law of *span of attention*
C. determined by the type of work supervised
D. fixed at not more than six

22. Of the following devices used in personnel administration, the MOST basic is 22.____

A. classification
B. service rating
C. appeals
D. in-service training

23. Of the following, the LEAST important factor for sound organization is the 23.____

A. individual and his position
B. hierarchical form of organization
C. location and delegation of authority
D. standardization of salary schedules

24. *Stretch–out* is a term that originated with the 24.____

A. imposition of a furlough
B. system of semi–monthly relief payments
C. development of labor technology
D. irregular development of low–cost housing projects

25. The one of the following which is LEAST generally true of a personnel division in a large department is that it is 25.____

A. concerned with having a certain point of view on personnel permeate the executive staff
B. charged with aiding operating executives with auxiliary staff service, assistance and advice
C. charged to administer a certain few operating duties of its own
D. charged with the basic responsibility for the efficient operation of the entire department

---

KEY (CORRECT ANSWERS)

1. A
2. C
3. A
4. B
5. B

6. D
7. B
8. D
9. C
10. C

11. D
12. C
13. C
14. A
15. B

16. A
17. C
18. D
19. B
20. D

21. C
22. A
23. D
24. C
25. D

TEST 2

Questions 1-10.

DIRECTIONS: Below are ten words numbered 1 through 10 and twenty other words divided into four groups - Group A, Group B, Group C and Group D. For each of the ten numbered words, select the word in one of the four groups which is MOST NEARLY the same in meaning. The letter of that group is the answer for the item. *PRINT THE LETTER OF THE CORRECT ANSWER IN THE SPACE AT THE RIGHT.*

1. abnegation 1.____
2. calumnious 2.____
3. purview 3.____
4. lugubrious 4.____
5. hegemony 5.____
6. arrogation 6.____
7. coalescence 7.____
8. prolix 8.____
9. syllogistic 9.____
10. contumely 10.____

GROUP A	GROUP B	GROUP C	GROUP D
articulation	bituminous	assumption	scope
fusion	deductive	forecast	vindication
catastrophic	repudiation	terse	amortization
inductive	doleful	insolence	productive
leadership	prolonged	panorama	slanderous

Questions 11-25.

DIRECTIONS: Each question or incomplete statement is followed by several suggested answers or completions. Select the one that BEST answers the question or completes the statement.

11. In large cities the total cost of government is of course *greater* than in small cities but 11.____

   A. this is accompanied by a decrease in per capita cost
   B. the per capita cost is also greater
   C. the per capita cost is approximately the same
   D. the per capita cost is considerably less in approximately 50% of the cases

12. The one of the following which is LEAST characteristic of governmental reorganizations is the 12.____

   A. saving of large sums of money
   B. problem of morale and personnel
   C. task of logic and management
   D. engineering approach

13. The LEAST accurate of the following statements about graphic presentation is 13.____

A. it is desirable to show as many coordinate lines as possible in a finished diagram
B. the horizontal scale should read from left to right and the vertical scale from top to bottom
C. when two or more curves are represented for comparison on the same chart, their zero lines should coincide
D. a percentage curve should not be used when the purpose is to show the actual amounts of increase or decrease

14. Grouping of figures in a frequency distribution results in a *loss* of 14.____

A. linearity B. significance C. detail D. coherence

15. The true financial condition of a city is BEST reflected when its accounting system is placed upon a(n) 15.____

A. cash basis B. accrual basis
C. fiscal basis D. warrant basis

16. When the discrepancy between the totals of a trial balance is $36, the LEAST probable cause of the error is 16.____

A. omission of an item
B. entering of an item on the wrong side of the ledger
C. a mistake in addition or subtraction
D. transposition of digits

17. For the *most effective* administrative management, appropriations should be 17.____

A. itemized B. lump sum C. annual D. bi-annual

18. Of the following types of expenditure control in the practice of fiscal management, the one which is LEAST important is that which relates to 18.____

A. past policy affecting expenditures
B. future policy affecting expenditures
C. prevention of improper use of funds
D. prevention of overdraft

19. The sinking fund method of retiring bonds does NOT 19.____

A. permit investment in a new issue of city bonds when the general market is unsatisfactory
B. cause irreparable injury to the city's credit when the city is unable to make a scheduled contribution
C. require periodic actuarial computations
D. cost as much to administer as the serial bond method

20. Of the following, the statement that is FALSE is: 20.____

A. Non-profit hospitalization plans are based on underlying principles similar to those which underlie mutual insurance
B. Federal, state and local governments pay for more than half of the medical care received by more than half of the population of the country
C. In addition to non-profit hospitalization, non-profit organizations providing reimbursement for medical and nursing care are now being organized in this state
D. Voluntary health insurance must be depended on since a state system of health insurance is unconstitutional

21. The *most accurate* of the following statements concerning birth and death rates is: 21.____

A. A high birth rate is usually accompanied by a relatively high death rate
B. A high birth rate is usually accompanied by a relatively low death rate
C. The rate of increase in population for a given area may be obtained by subtracting the death rate from the birth rate
D. The rate of increase in population for a given area may be obtained by subtracting the birth rate from the death rate

22. Empirical reasoning is based upon 22.____

A. experience and observation
B. *a priori* propositions
C. application of an established generalization
D. logical deduction

23. 45% of the employees of a certain department are enrolled in in-service training courses and 35% are registered in college courses. 23.____
The percentage of employees NOT enrolled in either of these types of courses is

A. 20%
B. at least 20% and not more than 55%
C. approximately 40%
D. none of these

24. A typist can address approximately R envelopes in a 7-hour day. A list containing S addresses is submitted with a request that all envelopes be typed within T hours. 24.____
The number of typists needed to complete this task would be

A. $\frac{7RS}{T}$
B. $\frac{S}{7RT}$
C. $\frac{R}{7ST}$
D. $\frac{7S}{RT}$

25. Bank X allows a customer to write without charge five checks per month for each $100 on deposit, but a check deposited or a cash deposit counts the same as a check written. Bank Y charges ten cents for every check written, requires no minimum balance and allows deposit of cash or of checks made out to customer free. A man receives two salary checks and, on the average, five other checks each month. He pays, on the average, twelve bills a month, five of which are for amounts between $5 and $10, five for amounts between $10 and $20, two for about $30. Assume that he pays these bills either by check or by Post Office money order (the charges for money orders are: $3.01 to $10–11¢; $10.01 to $20–13¢; $20.01 to $40–15¢) and that he has a savings account paying 2%. Assume also that if he has an account at Bank X, he keeps a balance sufficient to avoid any service charges. Of the following statements in relation to this man, the one that is TRUE is that 25.____

A. the monthly cost of an account at Bank Y is approximately as great as the cost of an account at Bank X and also the account is more convenient
B. to use an account at Bank Y costs more than the use of money orders, but this disadvantage is offset by the fact that cancelled checks act as receipts for bills paid
C. money orders are cheapest but this advantage is offset by the fact that one must go to the Post Office for each order
D. an account at Bank X is least expensive and has the advantage that checks endorsed to the customer may be deposited in it

KEY (CORRECT ANSWERS)

1. B
2. D
3. D
4. B
5. A
6. C
7. A
8. B
9. B
10. C
11. B
12. A
13. A
14. C
15. B
16. C
17. B
18. A
19. B
20. D
21. A
22. A
23. B
24. D
25. D

EXAMINATION SECTION
TEST 1

DIRECTIONS: Each question or incomplete statement is followed by several suggested answers or completions. Select the one that BEST answers the question or completes the statement. *PRINT THE LETTER OF THE CORRECT ANSWER IN THE SPACE AT THE RIGHT.*

1. Competent civil service personnel cannot come just from initial employment on a competitive basis and equal pay for equal work. 1.____
The one of the following additional factors which is of GREATEST importance in building up a body of competent civil service employees is

   A. analysis of work methods and introduction of streamlined procedures
   B. training for skill improvement and creating a sense of belonging
   C. rotation of employees from organization to organization in order to prevent stagnation
   D. treating personnel problems on a more impersonal basis in order to maintain an objective viewpoint
   E. recruiting for all higher positions from among the body of present employees

2. A comment made by an employee about a training course was: *Half of the group seem to know what the course is about, the rest of us can't keep up with them.* 2.____
The FUNDAMENTAL error in training methods to which this criticism points is

   A. insufficient student participation
   B. failure to develop a feeling of need or active want for the material being presented
   C. that the training session may be too long
   D. that no attempt may have been made to connect the new material with what was already known by any member of the group
   E. that insufficient provision has been made by the instructor for individual differences

3. The one of the following which is NOT a major purpose of an employee suggestion plan is to 3.____

   A. provide an additional method by means of which an employee's work performance can be evaluated
   B. increase employee interest in the work of the organization
   C. provide an additional channel of communication between the employee and top management
   D. utilize to the greatest extent possible the ideas and proposals of employees
   E. provide a formal method for rewarding the occasional valuable idea

4. The pay plan is a vital aspect of a duties classification. In fact, in most areas of personnel administration, pay plan and classification are synonymous. 4.____
This statement is

   A. *correct* in general; while the two are not, in general, synonymous, the pay plan is such a vital aspect that without it the classification plan is meaningless and useless
   B. *not correct;* while the pay plan is a vital aspect of a classification plan, it is not the only one

C. *correct* in general; pay plan and duties classification are simply two different aspects of the same problem - *equal pay for equal work*
D. *not correct;* although classification is usually a vital element of a pay plan, a pay plan is not essential to the preparation of a duties classification
E. *meaningless* unless the specific nature of the classification plan and the pay plan are set forth

5. The one of the following objectives which is MOST characteristic of intelligent personnel management is the desire to 5.____

A. obtain competent employees, and having them to provide the climate which will be most conducive to superior performance, proper attitudes, and harmonious adjustments
B. coordinate the activities of the workers in an organization so that the output will be maximized and cost minimized
C. reduce the dependence of an organization on the sentiments, ambitions, and idiosyncracies of individual employees and thus advance the overall aims of the organization
D. recruit employees who can be trained to subordinate their interests to the interests of the organization and to train them to do so
E. mechanize the procedures involved so that problems of replacement and training are reduced to a minimum

6. An organizational structure which brings together, in a single work unit, work divisions which are non-homogeneous in work, in technology, or in purpose will tend to decrease the danger of friction. 6.____
This opinion is, in general,

A. *correct;* individious comparisons tend to be made when everyone is doing the same thing
B. *not correct;* a homogeneous organization tends to develop a strong competitive spirit among its employees
C. *correct;* work which is non-homogeneous tends to be of greater interest to the employee, resulting in less friction
D. *not correct;* persons performing the same type of work tend to work together more efficiently
E. *correct;* the presence of different kinds of work permits better placement of employees, resulting in better morale

7. Of the following, the MOST accurate statement of current theory concerning the ultimate responsibility for employee training is that 7.____

A. ultimate responsibility for training is best separated from responsibility for production and administration
B. ultimate responsibility for training should be in the hands of a training specialist in the central personnel agency
C. a committee of employees selected from the trainees should be given ultimate responsibility for the training program
D. a departmental training specialist should be assigned ultimate responsibility for employee training
E. each official should be ultimately responsible for the training of all employees under his direction

8. The BEST of the following ways to reduce the errors in supervisors' ratings of employee performance caused by variations in the application of the rating standards is to 8.____

A. construct a method for translating each rating into a standard score
B. inform each supervisor of the distribution of ratings expected in his unit
C. review and change any rating which does not seem justified by the data presented by the rating supervisor
D. arrange for practice sessions for supervisors at which rating standards will be applied and discussed
E. confer with the supervisor when a case of disagreement is discovered between supervisor and review board

9. Which capsule description, among the following, constitutes an optimum arrangement of the hierarchical organization of a large-city central personnel agency? 9.____

A. Three commissioners who appoint a Director of Personnel to carry out the administrative functions but who handle the quasi-judicial and quasi-legislative duties themselves
B. A Director of Personnel and two Commissioners all three of whom participate in all aspects of the agency's functions
C. A Director of Personnel who is responsible for making the final decision in all matters pertaining to personnel administration in a city
D. A Director of Personnel who is the chief administrator and two Commissioners who, together with the Director, handle the quasi-judicial and quasi-legislative duties
E. Three Commissioners who have review powers over the acts of the Director of Personnel who is appointed on the basis of a competitive examination

10. The one of the following which is a major objective expected to be gained by setting up a personnel council composed of representatives of the central personnel agency and departmental personnel officers is to 10.____

A. provide an appeal board to which employees who feel grieved can appeal
B. allow the departments to participate in making the day-to-day decisions faced by the central personnel agency
C. prevent the departments from participating in making the day-to-day decisions faced by the central personnel agency
D. establish good communications between the central personnel agency and the departments
E. develop a broad base of responsibility for the actions of the central personnel agency

11. The one of the following which should be the starting point in the development of an accident reduction or prevention program is the 11.____

A. institution of an interorganizational safety contest
B. improvement of the conditions of work so that accidents are prevented
C. inauguration of a safety education program to reduce accidents due to carelessness
D. organization of unit safety committees to bring home the importance of safety to the individual worker
E. determination of the number, character, and causes of accidents

12. An orientation program for a group of new employees would NOT usually include 12.____

A. a description of the physical layout of the organization
B. a statement of the rules pertaining to leave, lateness, overtime, and so forth
C. detailed instruction on the job each employee is to perform
D. an explanation of the lines of promotion
E. a talk on the significance of the role the department plays in the governmental structure

13. The device of temporary assignment of an employee to the duties of the higher position is sometimes used to determine promotability. 13.____
The use of this procedure, especially for top positions, is

A. *desirable;* no test or series of tests can measure fitness to the same extent as actual trial on the job
B. *undesirable;* the organization will not have a responsible head during the trial period
C. *desirable;* employees who are on trial tend to operate with greater efficiency
D. *undesirable*; the organization would tend to deteriorate if no one of the candidates for the position was satisfactory
E. *desirable;* the procedure outlined is simpler and less expensive than any series of tests

14. Frequently, when accumulating data for a salary standardization study, the salaries for certain basic positions are compared with the salaries paid in other agencies, public and private. 14.____
The one of the following which would MOST usually be considered one of these basic positions is

A. Office Manager
B. Administrative Assistant
C. Chief Engineer
D. Junior Typist
E. Chemist

15. The emphasis in public personnel administration during recent years has been less on the 15.____

A. need for the elimination of the spoils system and more on the development of policy and techniques of administration that contribute to employee selection and productivity
B. development of policy and techniques of administration that contribute to employee selection and productivity and more on the need for the elimination of the spoils system
C. human relation aspects of personnel administration and more on the technical problems of classification and placement
D. problems of personnel administration of governmental units in the United States and more on those of international organizations
E. problems of personnel administration in international organizations and more on those of governmental units in the United States

16. The recommendation has been made that explicit information be made available to all city employees concerning the procedure to be followed when appealing from a performance rating. 16.____
To put this recommendation into effect would be

A. *desirable*, primarily because employees would tend to have greater confidence in the performance rating system
B. *undesirable*, primarily because a greater number of employees would submit appeals with no merit
C. *desirable*, primarily because the additional publicity would spotlight the performance rating system
D. *undesirable*, primarily because all appeals should be treated as confidential matters and all efforts to make them public should be defeated
E. *desirable*, primarily because committing the appeal procedure to paper would tend to standardize it

17. The one of the following which in most cases is the BEST practical measure of the merits of the overall personnel policies of one organization as compared to the policies of similar organizations in the same area is the 17.____

A. extent to which higher positions in the hierarchy are filled by career employees
B. degree of loyalty and enthusiasm manifested by the work force
C. rate at which replacements must be made in order to maintain the work force
D. percentage of employees who have joined labor unions and the militancy of these unions
E. scale of salaries

18. Classification may most properly be viewed as the building of a structure. The fundamental unit in the classification structure is the 18.____

A. assignment B. position C. service
D. rank E. grade

19. The one of the following which is NOT usually included in a class specification is 19.____

A. a definition of the duties and responsibilities covered
B. the class title
C. a description of the recruitment method to be used
D. a statement of typical tasks performed
E. the statement of minimum qualifications necessary to perform the work

20. The one of the following which is usually NOT considered part of a classification survey is 20.____

A. grouping positions on the basis of similarities
B. preparing job specifications
C. analyzing and recording specific job duties
D. adjusting job duties to employee qualifications
E. allocating individual positions to classes

21. The one of the following which is MOST generally accepted as a prerequisite to the development of a sound career service is 21.____

A. agreement to accept for all higher positions the senior eligible employee
B. the recruitment of an adequate proportion of beginning employees who will eventually be capable of performing progressively more difficult duties
C. strict adherence to the principle of competitive promotion from within for all positions above the entrance level

D. the development of a program of periodically changing an employee's duties in order to prevent stagnation
E. the existence of administrators who can stimulate employees and keep their production high

22. The determination of the fitness of a person to fill a position solely on the basis of his experience is 22.____

A. *desirable;* experience is the best test of aptitude for a position when it is rated properly
B. *undesirable;* the applicant may not be giving correct factual information in regard to his experience
C. *desirable;* a uniform rating key can be applied to evaluate experience
D. *undesirable;* it is difficult to evaluate from experience records how much the applicant has gained from his experience
E. *desirable;* there will be more applicants for a position if no written or oral tests are required

23. The performance rating standards in a city department have been criticized by its employees as unfair. 23.____
The one of the following procedures which would probably be HOST effective in reducing this criticism is to

A. publish a detailed statement showing how the standards were arrived at
B. provide for participation by employee representatives in revising the standards
C. allow individual employees to submit written statements about the standards employed
D. arrange for periodic meetings of the entire staff at which the standards are discussed
E. appoint a review board consisting of senior supervisory employees to reconsider the standards

24. The statement has been made that personnel administration is the MOST fundamental and important task of the head of any organization. 24.____
This statement is based, for the most part, on the fact that

A. success or failure of an organization to reach its objectives depends on the attitudes and abilities of the people in the organization
B. the influence of personnel administration on organization success varies in proportion to the number, the complexity, and the rarity of the virtues and qualities that are requisite to superior performance of the tasks involved
C. a sound philosophy of personnel administration emphasizes the basic objective of superior service over any other consideration
D. relative autonomy is permitted each department, particularly with respect to the handling of personnel
E. diversity of personnel practices as to salaries, hours, etc., leads to poor morale

25. The requirement imposed by most civil service laws in the United States that tests shall be *practical in character and deal in so far as possible with the actual duties of the position,* has led to a wide use of 25.____

A. tests of social outlook
B. aptitude tests
C. achievement tests
D. objective tests
E. oral tests

26. In general, the one of the following which is the first step in the construction of a test for the selection of personnel is to 26.____

A. determine what the duties of the position to be filled are
B. investigate the relationships among abilities and capacities required for success in the position to be filled
C. study examinations which have been given in the' past for similar positions
D. evaluate existing examining instruments to determine their adequacy for making the desired selection
E. set up the outline and start preliminary preparation of the examining instruments

27. The one of the following situations which is MOST likely to result from a too highly specified assignment or definition of responsibility is that 27.____

A. there will be no standard against which to measure the efficiency of the organization
B. duplication and overlapping of functions will be encouraged
C. sufficient channels to collect, synthesize, and coordinate all performances may not be provided
D. essential tasks which have not been explicitly mentioned in the assignment may not get done
E. there will be a tendency to overlook the need for training

28. Assume that you are interviewing a new entrance level clerical employee for the purpose of determining where he would be best placed. 28.____
In making your determination, the characteristic to which you should give GREATEST weight is the employee's

A. interest in the jobs you describe to him
B. mechanical aptitude
C. poise and self-assurance
D. fluency of verbal expression
E. educational background and his hobbies

29. The use of the probationary period in the public service has become an approved practice especially where state tenure laws guarantee long-term continuous employment. Of the following, the MOST important use of the probationary period is that it 29.____

A. provides supervisory contact which will help the new employee regardless of retention at the end of the probationary period
B. supplies confirming evidence of academic and cultural fitness not measurable in formal test procedures
C. introduces the new employee to the office and the work situation which conditions future performance
D. provides the new employee with a sound basis for self-improvement
E. reveals aspects of performance and attitude toward the job not adequately measured by formal examination

30. The first prerequisite to the formulation of any compensation plan for a public agency is the collection and analysis of certain basic data. 30.____
Data are NOT usually collected for this purpose in regard to

A. working conditions in the agency
B. the wage paid in the agency at present
C. labor turnover in the agency
D. the cost of living in the area
E. the age and sex distribution of the employees

31. The one of the following personnel administration techniques which when properly utilized will yield information concerning current training needs of an organization is the 31.____

A. classification plan
B. performance rating
C. personnel register
D. compensation plan
E. employee handbook

32. In administering the activities of a personnel office with a staff of fifteen employees, including seven personnel technicians, the personnel officer should 32.____

A. delegate full authority and responsibility to each staff member and discharge those who do not meet his standards
B. endeavor to keep tab on the work of each individual on his staff
C. make sure each job is being done properly or do it himself
D. plan work programs, make assignments, and check on performance
E. concern himself only with major policies and expect subordinates to carry out actual functions

33. The one of the following factors which is MOST influential in determining the proportion of qualified applicants who refuse public employment when offered is the 33.____

A. interim between application and offer of a position
B. specific nature of the duties of the position
C. general nature of economic conditions at the time when the position is offered
D. salary paid
E. general undesirable nature of public employment

34. A placement officer in a department follows the procedure of consulting the supervisor of the unit in which a vacancy exists concerning the kind of worker he wants before attempting to fill the vacancy. 34.____
This procedure is, in general,

A. *undesirable;* it makes the selection process dependent on the whim of the supervisor
B. *desirable;* it will make for a more effectively working organization
C. *undesirable;* if the kind of worker the supervisor wants is not available, he will be dissatisfied
D. *desirable;* the more people who are consulted about a matter of this kind, the more chance there is that no mistake will be made
E. *undesirable;* the wishes of the worker as well as those of the supervisor should be taken into consideration

35. In a large organization, proper recruitment is not possible without the existence of an effective position classification system. 35.____
The one of the following which BEST explains why this is the case is that otherwise effective means of determining the capabilities and characteristics of prospective employees are of little value

A. unless these are related to the salary scale and current economic conditions
B. without a knowledge of the essential character of the work to be performed in each position
C. where no attempt to classify the different recruitment approaches has been made in advance
D. if there has been no attempt made to obtain the cooperation of the employees involved
E. to personnel officers who tend to place new employees in positions without reference to capabilities

36. The recommendation has been made that a departmental grievance board be set up, which would handle all employee grievances from their inception to conclusion. 36.____
Of the following comments for and against the acceptance of this recommendation, the one which is NOT valid is that it is

A. *desirable,* primarily because it will remove a constant source of friction between supervisor and employee and place the problem in the hands of an objective board
B. *undesirable,* primarily because handling grievances is an integral part of the supervisory process and the immediate supervisor must be afforded the opportunity to deal with the situation
C. *desirable,* primarily because no supervisor will have to determine whether he has been unfair to one of his subordinates and no subordinate will have a grievance
D. *desirable,* primarily because the handling of grievances will tend to be expedited as the board will have only one function
E. *undesirable,* primarily because the handling of grievances will tend to be delayed as the board will not have all the necessary information available

37. The one of the following which is frequently given as a major argument against a tightly knit promotion-from-within policy is that 37.____

A. it takes too long for an employee in the lower grades to reach the top
B. all persons both in and out of the government are equally entitled to civil service jobs
C. persons are placed in executive jobs who are too well acquainted with the existing organization
D. it leads to the presence in executive jobs of clerks who still operate as clerks
E. it is not desirable to guarantee to all employees promotion to new responsibilities from time to time

38. Of the following factors which are influential in determining which employment a young man or woman will choose, government employ is generally considered superior in 38.____

A. incentives to improve efficiency
B. opportunities to move into other similar organizations
C. prestige and recognition
D. leave and retirement benefits
E. salaries

39. Training programs, to be fully effective, should be concerned not only with the acquisition or improvement of skills but also with 39.____

A. employee attitude and will to work
B. the personality problems of the individual employees
C. time and motion studies for the development of new procedures
D. the recruitment of the best persons available to fill a given position
E. such theoretical background material as is deemed necessary

Questions 40-45.

DIRECTIONS: Questions 40 through 45 are to be answered on the basis of the following paragraphs.

Plan 1 Hire broadly qualified people, work out their assignments from time to time to suit the needs of the enterprise and aptitudes of individuals. Let their progress and recognition be based on the length and overall quality of the service, regardless of the significance of individual assignments which they periodically assume.

Plan 2 Hire experts and assign them well-defined duties. Their compensation, for the most part, should be dependent on the duties performed.

40. For Plan 1 to be successful, there must be assured, to a much greater extent than for Plan 2, the existence of 40.____

A. a well-developed training program
B. a widely publicized recruitment program
C. in general, better working conditions
D. more skilled administrators
E. a greater willingness to work together toward a common goal

41. Plan 1 would tend to develop employees who were 41.____

A. dissatisfied because of the impossibility of advancing rapidly to positions of importance
B. conversant only with problems in the particular field in which they were employed
C. in general, not satisfied with the work they perform
D. intensely competitive
E. able to perform a variety of functions

42. Large governmental organizations in the United States tend, in general, to use Plan 42.____

A. 1
B. 2
C. 1 for technical positions and Plan 2 for clerical positions
D. 2 for administrative positions and Plan 1 for clerical and technical positions
E. 1 for office machine operators and Plan 2 for technical positions

43. In organizations which operate on the basis of Plan 1, placement of a man in the proper job after selection is much more difficult than in those which operate on the basis of Plan 2. 43.____
This statement is, in general,

A. *correct;* the organization would have only specific positions open and generalists would be forced into technical positions
B. *not correct;* specific aptitudes and abilities would tend to be determined in advance as would be the case with Plan 2
C. *correct;* it is much more difficult to determine specific aptitudes and abilities than general qualifications
D. *not correct;* placement would be based on the needs of the organization, consequently only a limited number of positions would be available
E. *correct;* the selection is not on the basis of specific aptitudes and abilities

44. Administration in an organization operating on the basis of Plan 1 would tend to be less flexible than one operating on the basis of Plan 2. 44.____
This statement is, in general,

A. *correct;* recruitment of experts permits rapid expansion
B. *not correct;* the absence of well-defined positions permits wide and rapid recruitment without an extensive selection period
C. *correct;* well-defined positions allow for replacement on an assembly-line basis without an extensive breaking-in period and thus permits greater flexibility
D. *not correct;* Plan 1 presents greater freedom in movement of individuals from one position to another and in re-defining positions according to capabilities of employees and the needs of the moment
E. *correct;* Plan 1 presents greater freedom in adjusting an organizational structure to unexpected stresses since the clear definition of duties shows where the danger points are

45. To a greater extent than Plan 2, Plan 1 leads to conflict and overlapping in administrative operations. 45.____
In general, this is the case because

A. employees paid on the basis of duties performed tend to be more conscious of overlapping operations and tend to limit their activities
B. experts refuse to accept responsibilities in fields other than their own
C. the lack of carefully defined positions may conceal many points at which coordination and reconciliation are necessary
D. there tends to be more pressure for *empire building* where prestige is measured solely in terms of assignment
E. there is less need, under Plan 1, to define lines of responsibility and authority and consequently conflict will arise

46. Some organizations interview employees who resign or are discharged. 46.____
This procedure is USUALLY

A. of great value in reducing labor turnover and creating good will toward the organization
B. of little or no value as the views of incompetent or disgruntled employees are of questionable validity

C. dangerous; it gives employees who are leaving an organization the opportunity to pay off old scores
D. of great value in showing the way to more efficient methods of production and the establishment of higher work norms
E. dangerous; it may lead to internal friction as operating departments believe that it is not the function of the personnel office to check on operations

47. The one of the following which is the MOST common flaw in the administration of an employee performance rating system is the 47.____

A. failure to explain the objectives of the system to employees
B. lack of safeguards to prevent supervisors from rating employees down for personal reasons
C. tendency for rating supervisors to rate their employees much too leniently
D. fact that employees are aware of the existence of the system
E. increasing number of committees and boards required

48. As a result of its study of the operations of the Federal government, the Hoover Commission recommended that, for purposes of reduction in force, employees be ranked from the standpoint of their overall usefulness to the agency in question. 48.____
The one of the following which is a major disadvantage of this proposal is that it would probably result in

A. efficient employees becoming indifferent to the social problems posed
B. a sense of insecurity on the part of employees which might tend to lower efficiency
C. the retention of employees who are at or just past their peak performance
D. the retention of generalists rather than specialists
E. the loss of experience in the agency, as ability rather than knowledge will be the criterion

49. A personnel officer checking the turnover rate in his department found that, over a period of five years, the rate at which engineers left the organization was exactly the same as the rate at which junior clerks left the department. 49.____
This information tends to indicate

A. that something may be amiss with the organization; the rate for engineers under ordinary circumstances should be higher than for clerks
B. that the organization is in good shape; neither the technical nor clerical aspects are being overemphasized
C. nothing which would be of value in determining the state of the organization
D. that the organization is in good shape; working conditions, in general, are equivalent for all employees
E. that something may be amiss with the organization; the turnover rate for engineers under ordinary circumstances should be lower than for clerks

50. Of the following, the MOST essential feature of a grievance procedure is that 50.____

A. those who appeal be assured of expert counsel
B. the administration have opportunity to review cases early in the procedure
C. it afford assurance that those who use it will not be discriminated against
D. general grievances be publicized
E. it be simple to administer

KEY (CORRECT ANSWERS)

1.	B	11.	E	21.	B	31.	B	41.	E
2.	E	12.	C	22.	D	32.	D	42.	B
3.	A	13.	A	23.	B	33.	A	43.	E
4.	D	14.	D	24.	A	34.	B	44.	D
5.	A	15.	A	25.	C	35.	B	45.	C
6.	D	16.	A	26.	A	36.	B	46.	A
7.	E	17.	C	27.	D	37.	D	47.	C
8.	D	18.	B	28.	A	38.	D	48.	B
9.	D	19.	C	29.	E	39.	A	49.	E
10.	D	20.	D	30.	E	40.	A	50.	C

TEST 2

DIRECTIONS: Each question or incomplete statement is followed by several suggested answers or completions. Select the one that BEST answers the question or completes the statement. *PRINT THE LETTER OF THE CORRECT ANSWER IN THE SPACE AT THE RIGHT.*

1. In which of the following fields could two or more groups duplicating each other's work USUALLY be best justified? 1.____

   A. Accounting
   B. Personnel
   C. Public relations
   D. Research and development
   E. Systems and procedures

2. Which of the following statements is MOST nearly accurate? A span of control 2.____

   A. of 5 people is better than that of 10 people
   B. of 5 people may be better or worse than that of 10 people
   C. of 5 people is worse than that of 10 people
   D. is rarely over 20 minutes at any one time
   E. means the same as the scalar system

3. A linear responsibility chart is 3.____

   A. a graphical method of showing each sub-project making up a total project with the time it takes to complete each
   B. a graphical method of showing jobs, functions, and, by the use of appropriate symbols, the relationship of each job to each function
   C. a graphical method of solving linear equations used in doing Operations Research
   D. a new method of procedures analysis which makes it possible to focus on both the employees and the equipment they use
   E. another name for a special organization chart

4. An administrator of a public agency is faced with the problem of deciding which of two divisions should be responsible for the statistical reporting of the agency. This work is now located in one of them but each of the two division chiefs believes that the work should be located within his division because of its relationship to other activities under his supervision. The Organization Planning Section is located in one of the two divisions. Assuming that in this situation the administrator can select any one of the following courses of action, the BEST for him to take would be to 4.____

   A. assign a staff member from the Organization Planning Section to study the problem, who for the duration of the assignment would report directly to the administrator
   B. assign staff from the Organization Planning Section to study the problem
   C. assign the statistical work to the other division for a trial period because of the problems which exist under the present arrangement
   D. call in an outside consultant or refer it to a competent staff employee not assigned to the divisions involved
   E. leave the organization as it is because the advantages of a change are not entirely clear to all concerned

5. The problem of whether office services such as filing, duplicating, and stenography should be centralized or decentralized arises in every business organization. One advantage of decentralizing these services is that 5.____

A. greater facility exists in such matters as finding correspondence
B. greater flexibility exists in rotating workers during vacations
C. higher production is attained at a lower cost per unit
D. knowledge of the purpose and use of work acts as an incentive for production
E. reduction in investment results from the use of less machinery

6. Research to date on the relationship between productivity and morale shows that 6.____

A. high productivity and high morale nearly always go together
B. high productivity and low morale nearly always go together
C. low productivity and high morale nearly always go together
D. low productivity and low morale nearly always go together
E. there is no clear relationship between productivity and morale

7. Which one of the following statements BEST describes *work measurement* as commonly used in government? It is 7.____

A. a method of establishing an equitable relationship between volume of work performed and manpower utilized
B. a new technique which may be substituted for traditional accounting methods
C. the amount of work turned out by an organization in a given time period
D. the same as the work count, as used in Work Simplification
E. the same as time-motion study

8. Critics of work measurement have contended that any increase in production is more than offset by deterioration in standards of quality or service. The BEST answer to this charge is to 8.____

A. argue that increases in production have not been offset by decreased quality
B. define work units in terms of both quality and quantity
C. ignore it
D. point out that statistical quality control can be used to control quality
E. point out that work measurement is not concerned with quality, and hence that the argument is irrelevant

9. When it is determined that a given activity or process is so intangible that it cannot be reflected adequately by a work unit, it is BEST for a work measurement system to 9.____

A. combine that activity with others that are measurable
B. discuss the activity only in narrative reports
C. exclude it from the work measurement system
D. include only the time devoted to that activity or process
E. select the best available work unit, as better than none

10. Which one of the following is frequently referred to as the father of Statistical Quality Control? 10.____

A. Ralph M. Barnes
B. John M. Pfiffner
C. Benjamin Selekman
D. Walter A. Shewhart
E. Donald C. Stone

11. Which one of the following BEST explains the use and value of the *upper control limit* (and *lower control limit* where applicable) in Statistical Quality Control? 11.____
It

A. automatically keeps production under control
B. indicates that unit costs are too high or too low
C. is useful as a training device for new workers
D. tells what pieces to discard or errors to correct
E. tells when assignable causes as distinguished from chance causes are at work

12. A manager skilled in human relations can BEST be defined as one who 12.____

A. can identify interpersonal problems and work out solutions to them
B. can persuade people to do things his way
C. gets along well with people and has many friends
D. plays one role with his boss, another with his subordinates, and a third with his peers
E. treats everyone fairly

13. The BEST way to secure efficient management is to 13.____

A. allow staff agencies to solve administrative problems
B. equip line management to solve its own problems
C. get employees properly classified and trained
D. prescribe standard operating procedures
E. set up a board of control

14. The composition of the work force in American government and industry is changing. There has been an increase in the proportion of white collar to blue collar employees and an increase in the proportion of higher educated to lower educated employees. 14.____
This change will MOST likely result in

A. a more simplified forms control system
B. closer supervision of employees
C. further decentralization of decision-making
D. more employee grievances
E. organization by process instead of purpose

15. In which of the following professional journals would you be MOST apt to find articles on organization theory? 15.____

A. Administrative Science Quarterly
B. Factory Management and Maintenance
C. Harvard Business Review
D. O and M
E. Public Administration Review

16. Which of the following organizations is MOST noted for its training courses in various management subjects? 16.____

A. American Management Association
B. American Political Science Association
C. American Society for Public Administration
D. Society for the Advancement of Management
E. Systems and Procedures Association

17. A *performance budget* puts emphasis on 17.____

A. achieving greatest economy
B. expenditures for salaries, travel, rent, supplies, etc.
C. revenues rather than on expenditures
D. tables of organization or staffing patterns
E. what is accomplished, e.g., number of applications processed, trees planted, buildings inspected, etc.

18. Which of the following statements MOST accurately defines *Operations Research?* 18.____

A. A highly sophisticated reporting system used in the analysis of management problems
B. A specialized application of electronic data processing in the analysis of management problems
C. Research on operating problems
D. Research on technological problems
E. The application of sophisticated mathematical tools to the analysis of management problems

19. Which of the following characteristics of a system would MOST likely lead to the conclusion that manual methods should be used rather than punch card equipment? 19.____

A. High volume
B. Low volume but complex computations
C. Operations of a fixed sequence
D. Relatively simple work
E. Repetitive work

20. Assume that a computer with typing software costs $1100 and an electric typewriter costs $300. Except for speed of production, assume that in all other pertinent respects they are the same, including a life expectancy of 10 years each. 20.____
What is the approximate amount of time $7.40 per hour typist must save and re-invest in work to have her computer recoup the difference in purchase price?

A. 11 hours annually
B. 110 hours annually
C. 550 hours annually
D. 1100 hours annually
E. One hour a day

21. The principal justification for using office machines to replace hand labor is to 21.____

A. achieve automation
B. eliminate errors
C. increase productivity
D. make work easier
E. reduce labor problems

22. An analog computer is one which 22.____

A. is classified as *medium* size
B. is used primarily for solving scientific and engineering problems rather than for data processing
C. operates on the principle of creating a physical, often electrical, analogy of the mathematical problem to be solved
D. uses transistors rather than vacuum tubes
E. works on the basis of logarithms

23. The binary numbering system used in computers is one which 23.____

A. is much more complicated than the usual decimal numbering system
B. uses a radix or base of 8
C. uses letters of the alphabet rather than numerical digits
D. uses only two digits, 0 and 1
E. uses the customary ten digits, 0 through 9

24. An electronic computer performs various arithmetic operations by 24.____

A. adding and subtracting
B. adding, subtracting, dividing, and multiplying
C. Boolean algebra
D. multiplying and dividing
E. all operations listed in B and C

25. The MOST effective basis for an analysis of the flow of work in a large governmental agency is the 25.____

A. analysis of descriptions written by employees
B. discussion of routines with selected employees
C. discussion of operations with supervisors
D. initiation of a series of general staff meetings to discuss operational procedures
E. observation of actual operations

26. The BEST reason for prescribing definite procedures for certain work in an organization is to 26.____

A. enable supervisor to keep *on top of* details of work
B. enable work to be processed speedily and consistently
C. facilitate incorporation of new policies
D. prevent individual discretion
E. reduce training periods

27. Which one of the following is the MOST important difference between clerks in small offices and those in large offices? 27.____
Clerks in

A. large offices are less closely supervised
B. large offices have more freedom to exercise originality in their work
C. small offices are more restricted by standardized procedures
D. small offices are more specialized in their duties
E. small offices need a greater variety of clerical skills

28. After taking the necessary steps to analyze a situation, an employee reaches a decision which is reviewed by his supervisor and found to be incorrect. 28.____
Of the following possible methods of dealing with this incident, the MOST constructive for the employee would be for the supervisor to

A. correct the decision and give the employee an explanation
B. correct the decision and suggest more detailed analysis in the future
C. help the employee discover what is wrong with the basis for decision
D. set up a temporary control on this type of decision until the employee demonstrates he can handle it
E. suggest that the employee review future cases of this type with him before reaching a decision

29. Which one of the following is NOT a purpose ordinarily served by charts? 29.____

A. Aid in training employees
B. Assist in presenting and selling recommendations
C. Detect gaps or discrepancies in data collected
D. Put facts in proper relationships to each other
E. Show up problems of human relationships

30. Which of the following descriptive statements does NOT constitute a desirable standard in evaluating an administrative sequence or series of tasks having a definite objective? 30.____

A. All material should be routed as directly as possible to reduce the cost of time and motion.
B. Each form must clear the section chief before going to another section.
C. Each task should be assigned to the lowest-ranking employee who can perform it adequately.
D. Each task should contribute positively to the basic purpose of the sequence.
E. Similar tasks should be combined.

31. Which one of the following is NOT a principle of motion economy? 31.____

A. Continuous curved motions are preferable to straight-line motions involving sudden and sharp changes in direction.
B. Motions of the arms should be made in the same direction and should be made simultaneously.
C. The hands should be relieved of all work that can be performed more advantageously by the feet.
D. The two hands should begin and complete their motions at the same time.
E. Two or more tools should be combined whenever possible.

32. Generally, the first step in the measurement of relative efficiency of office employees engaged in machine operation is the 32.____

   A. analysis of the class of positions involved to determine the duties and responsibilities and minimum qualifications necessary for successful job performance
   B. analysis of those skills which make for difference in the production of various employees
   C. development of a service rating scale which can be scored accurately
   D. development of a standard unit of production that can be widely applied and that will give comparable data
   E. selection of an appropriate sampling of employees whose duties involve the specific factors to be measured

33. In the course of a survey, a disgruntled employee of Unit A comes to your office with an offer to *tell all* about Unit B, where he used to work. 33.____
You should

   A. listen to him but ignore any statements he makes
   B. listen to him carefully, but verify his assertions before acting on them
   C. make him speak to you in the presence of the persons he is criticizing
   D. reprimand him for not minding his own business
   E. report him to the security officer

34. Combining several different procedures into a single flow of work would MOST likely achieve which of the following advantages? 34.____

   A. Better teamwork
   B. Higher quality decisions
   C. Improved morale
   D. Reduced fluctuations in workload
   E. Reduced problems of control

35. After conducting a systems survey in the Personnel Division you find that there is not sufficient work in the Division to keep a recently hired employee gainfully employed. 35.____
The BEST solution to this problem is usually to

   A. lay off the employee with a full month's salary
   B. leave the employee in the Division because the workload may increase
   C. leave the employee in the Personnel Division, but assign him overflow work from other divisions
   D. reassign the employee when an appropriate opening occurs elsewhere in the organization
   E. request the employee to resign so that no unfavorable references will appear on his personnel record

36. You are making a study of a central headquarters office which processes claims received from a number of regional offices. You notice the following problems: some employees are usually busy while others assigned to the same kind of work in the same grade have little to do; high-level professional people frequently spend considerable time searching for files in the file room. 36.____
Which of the following charts would be MOST useful to record and analyze the data needed to help solve these problems?
_______ chart.

A. forms distribution
B. layout
C. operation
D. process
E. work distribution

37. A *therblig* is BEST defined as a 37.____

A. follower of Frederick W. Taylor
B. small element or task of an operation used in time-motion study
C. special type of accounting machine
D. type of curve used in charting certain mathematical relationships
E. unit for measuring the effectiveness of air conditioning

38. One of the following advantages which is LEAST likely to accrue to a large organization as a result of establishing a centralized typing and stenographic unit is that 38.____

A. less time is wasted
B. morale of the stenographers increases
C. the stenographers receive better training
D. wages are more consistent
E. work is more equally distributed

39. In the communications process, the work *noise* is used to refer to 39.____

A. anything that interferes with the message between transmitter and receiver
B. meaningless communications
C. the amplitude of verbal communication
D. the level of general office and environmental sounds other than specific verbal communications
E. the product of the grapevine

40. Which of the following is NOT an advantage of oral instructions as compared with written instructions when dealing with a small group? 40.____

A. Oral instructions are more adaptable to complex orders
B. Oral instructions can be changed more easily and quickly.
C. Oral instructions facilitate exchange of information between the order giver and order receiver.
D. Oral instructions make it easier for order giver and order receiver.
E. The oral medium is suitable for instructions that will be temporary.

41. The employee opinion or attitude survey has for some time been accepted as a valuable communications device. 41.____
Of the following, the benefit which is LEAST likely to occur from the use of such a survey is:

A. A clearer view of employee understanding of management policies is obtained
B. Improved morale may result
C. Information useful for supervisory and executive development is obtained
D. The reasons why management policies were adopted are clarified
E. Useful comparisons can be made between organization units

42. Which of the following is the MOST important principle to remember in preparing written reports that are to be submitted to a superior? 42.____

A. Avoid mentioning in writing errors or mistakes
B. Include human interest anecdotes
C. Put all information into graphical or tabular form
D. Report everything that has happened
E. Report results in relation to plan

43. In conducting an electronic data processing study, with which one of the following should you be LEAST concerned? 43.____

A. Computer characteristics; i.e., word length requirements, type storage characteristics, etc.
B. Data collection requirements
C. Methods used by other governmental jurisdictions
D. System input/output requirements and volume
E. System integration and flow of work

44. The MOST significant difference between a random access and a sequential type data processing computer system is 44.____

A. Generally, a random access system has lower *locating* or access times
B. Random access provides the potential for processing data on a *first come-first served* basis without the necessity of batching or pre-arranging the data in some sequence
C. Random access systems are more often disk type storage systems
D. Random access systems can operate more easily in conjunction with sequential tape or card oriented computer systems
E. Random access systems have larger storage capacities

45. The most effective leader would MOST likely be one who 45.____

A. is able to use a variety of leadership styles depending on the circumstances
B. issues clear, forceful directives
C. knows the substance of the work better than any of his subordinates
D. supervises his subordinates closely
E. uses democratic methods

46. One large office is a more efficient operating unit than the same number of square feet split into smaller offices. 46.____
Of the following, the one that does NOT support this statement is:

A. Better light and ventilation are possible
B. Changes in layout are less apt to be made thus avoiding disruption of work flow
C. Communication between individual employees is more direct
D. Space is more fully utilized
E. Supervision and control are more easily maintained

47. The major purpose for adopting specific space standards is to 47.____

A. allocate equal space to employees doing the same kind of work
B. cut costs
C. keep space from becoming a status symbol
D. prevent empire-building
E. provide an accurate basis for charging for space allocated to each organization unit

48. The modular concept in office space planning is 48.____

A. a method of pre-planning office space for economical use
B. expensive because it complicates the air conditioning and electrical systems
C. outdated because it lacks flexibility
D. used as a basis for planning future space requirements
E. used primarily for executive offices

49. Which one of the following statements is NOT correct? 49.____

A. A general conference or committee room may eliminate the need for a number of private offices.
B. In designing office space the general trend is toward the use of a standard color scheme.
C. Private offices should be constructed in such a way as to avoid cutting off natural light and ventilation.
D. Private offices result in a larger investment in equipment and furnishings.
E. Transparent or translucent glass can be used in the upper portion of the partition for private offices.

50. Which one of the following is NOT a good general rule of communications in an organization? 50.____

A. All supervisors should know the importance of communications.
B. Oral communications are better than written where persuasion is needed.
C. People should be told facts that make them feel they *belong.*
D. The grapevine should be eliminated.
E. The supervisor should hear information before his subordinates.

KEY (CORRECT ANSWERS)

1.	D	11.	E	21.	C	31.	B	41.	D
2.	B	12.	A	22.	C	32.	D	42.	E
3.	B	13.	B	23.	D	33.	B	43.	C
4.	D	14.	C	24.	A	34.	D	44.	B
5.	D	15.	A	25.	E	35.	D	45.	A
6.	E	16.	A	26.	B	36.	E	46.	B
7.	A	17.	E	27.	E	37.	B	47.	A
8.	B	18.	E	28.	C	38.	B	48.	A
9.	D	19.	B	29.	E	39.	A	49.	B
10.	D	20.	A	30.	B	40.	A	50.	D

EXAMINATION SECTION

TEST 1

DIRECTIONS: Each question or incomplete statement is followed by several suggested answers or completions. Select the one that BEST answers the question or completes the statement. *PRINT THE LETTER OF THE CORRECT ANSWER IN THE SPACE AT THE RIGHT.*

1. One of the major objectives of a pre-employment interview is to get the interviewee to respond freely to inquiries. 1.____
   The one of the following actions that would be MOST likely to restrict the conversation of the interviewee would be for the investigator to
   A. keep a stenographic record of the interviewee's statements
   B. ask questions requiring complete explanations
   C. pose direct, specific questions to the interviewee
   D. allow the interviewee to respond to questions at his own pace

2. One of the reasons for the widespread use of the interview in personnel selection is that the interview 2.____
   A. has been shown to be a valid measurement technique
   B. is efficient and reliable
   C. has been demonstrated to result in consistency among raters
   D. allows for flexibility of response

3. In conducting a personnel interview, which of the following guidelines would be MOST desirable for the interviewer to follow? 3.____
   A. Allocate the same amount of time to each person being interviewed to standardize the process
   B. Ask exactly the same questions of all persons being interviewed to increase the objectivity of the process
   C. Eliminate the use of non-directive techniques because of their subjectivity
   D. Vary his style and technique to fit the purpose of the interview and the people being interviewed

4. You are planning to conduct preliminary interviews of applicants for an important position in your department. 4.____
   Which of the following planning considerations is LEAST likely to contribute to successful interviews?
   A. Make provisions to conduct interviews in privacy
   B. Schedule your appointments so that interviews will be short
   C. Prepare a list of your objectives
   D. Learn as much as you can about the applicant before the interview

5. When dealing with an aggrieved worker, a USEFUL interviewing technique is to 5.____
   A. maintain a sympathetic attitude
   B. maintain an attitude of cold impartiality

C. assure the subject that you are on his side
D. display a tape recorder to give the subject confidence that no parts of his story will be overlooked

6. The "patterned interview" is a device used by sophisticated employers to 6.____
A. select employees who fit the ethnic pattern of the community
B. ascertain the pattern of facts surrounding a grievance
C. discourage workers from joining unions
D. appraises a subject's most important character traits

7. One of the applicants for a menial job is a tall, stooped, husky individual with a low forehead, narrow eyes, a protruding chin, and a tendency to keep his mouth open. 7.____
In interviewing him, you should
A. check him more carefully than the other applicants regarding criminal background
B. disregard any skills he might have for other jobs which are vacant
C. make your vocabulary somewhat simpler than with the other applicants
D. make no assumptions regarding his ability on the basis of his appearance

8. Of the following, the BEST approach for you to use at the beginning of an interview with a job applicant is to 8.____
A. caution him to use his time economically and to get to the point
B. ask him how long he intends to remain on the job if hired
C. make some pleasant remarks to put him at ease
D. emphasize the importance of the interview in obtaining the job

9. Of the following, the BEST reason for conducting an "exit interview" with an employee is to 9.____
A. make certain that he returns all identification cards and office keys
B. find out why he is leaving
C. provide a useful training device for the exit interviewer
D. discover if his initial hiring was in error

10. If you are to interview several applicants for jobs and rate them on five different factors on a scale of 1 to 5, you should be MOST careful to *insure* that your 10.____
A. rating on one factor does not influence your rating on another factor
B. ratings on all factors are interrelated with a minimum of variation
C. overall evaluation for employment exactly reflects the arithmetic average of your ratings
D. overall evaluation for employment is unrelated to your individual ratings

11. Of the following, the question MOST appropriate for initial screening purposes GENERALLY is: 11.____
A. What are your salary requirements?
B. Why do you think you would like this kind of work?
C. How did you get along with your last supervisor?
D. What are your vocational goals?

12. Of the following, normally the question MOST appropriate for selection purposes generally would tend to be: 12.____
    A. Where did you work last?
    B. When did you graduate from high school?
    C. What was your average in school?
    D. Why did you select this organization?

13. Assume that you have been asked to interview each of several students who have been hired to work part-time. 13.____
    Which of the following would ordinarily be accomplished LEAST effectively in such an interview?
    A. Providing information about the organization or institution in which the students will be working
    B. Directing the students to report for work each afternoon at specified times
    C. Determining experience and background of the students so that appropriate assignments can be made
    D. Changing the attitudes of the students toward the importance of parental controls

14. In interviewing job applicants, which of the following usually does NOT have to be done before the end of the interview? 14.____
    A. Making a decision to hire an applicant
    B. Securing information from applicants
    C. Giving information to applicants
    D. Establishing a friendly relationship with applicants

15. In the process of interviewing applicants for a position on your staff, the one of the following which would be BEST is to 15.____
    A. make sure all applicants are introduced to the other members of your staff prior to the formal interview
    B. make sure the applicant does not ask questions about the job or the department
    C. avoid having the applicant talk with the staff at the conclusion of a successful interview
    D. introduce applicants to some of the staff at the conclusion of a successful interview

16. While interviewing a job applicant, you ask applicant why he left his last job. The applicant does not answer immediately. 16.____
    Of the following, the BEST action to take at that point is to
    A. wait until he answers
    B. ask another question
    C. repeat the question in a loud voice
    D. ask him why he does not answer

17. You know that a student applying for a job in your office has done well in college except for two courses in science. However, when you ask him about his grades, his reply is vague and general. 17.____

It would be BEST for you to
A. lead the applicant to admitting doing poorly in science to be sure that the facts are correct
B. judge the applicant's tact and skill in handling what may be for him a personally sensitive question
C. immediately confront the applicant with the facts and ask for an explanation
D. ignore the applicant's response since you have the transcript

18. A college student has applied for a position with your department. 18.____
Prior to conducting an interview of the job applicant, it would be LEAST helpful for you to have
A. a personal resume
B. a job description
C. references
D. hiring requirements

19. Job applicants tend to be nervous during interviews. 19.____
Which of the following techniques is MOST likely to put such an applicant at ease?
A. Try to establish rapport by asking general questions which are easily answered by the applicant
B. Ask the applicant to describe his career objectives immediately, thus minimizing the anxiety caused by waiting
C. Start the interview with another member of the staff present so that the applicant does not feel alone
D. Proceed as rapidly as possible, since the emotional state of the applicant is none of your concern

20. At the first interview between a supervisor and a newly appointed subordinate, GREATEST care should be taken to 20.____
A. build toward a satisfactory personal relationship even if some other objectives of the interview must be postponed
B. cover a predetermined list of specific objectives so as to make a further orientation interview unnecessary
C. create an image of a forceful, determined supervisor whose wishes cannot be opposed by a subordinate without great risk
D. create an impression of efficiency and control of operation free from interpersonal relationships

21. You are a supervisor in an agency and are holding your first interview with a new employee. 21.____
In this interview, you should strive MAINLY to
A. show the new employee that you are an efficient and objective supervisor, with a completely impersonal attitude toward your subordinates
B. complete the entire orientation process including the giving of detailed job-duty instructions

C. make it clear to the employee that all your decisions are based on your many years of experience
D. lay the groundwork for a good employee-supervisor relationship by gaining the new employee's confidence

22. The INCORRECT statement related to the principles of interviewing is: 22.____
A. Written outlines should be avoided by the interviewer because they tend to be overly restrictive.
B. Preliminary planning (for the interview) should involve an analysis of the point of view of the person to be interviewed.
C. An interviewing supervisor should make every effort to conduct it in privacy to avoid possible inhibitions.
D. Well-planned questions are sometimes necessary in conducting an interview.

23. Assume that you are conducting an interview with a prospective employee who is of limited mental ability and low socio-economic status. 23.____
Of the following, it is MOST likely that asking him many open-ended questions about his work experience would cause him to respond
A. articulately B. reluctantly C. comfortably D. aggressively

24. An individual interview is to be used as part of an examination for a supervisory position. 24.____
Of the following, the attribute or characteristic that is LEAST suitable for evaluation in such an interview is
A. ability to supervise people
B. poise and confidence
C. response to stress conditions
D. rigidity and flexibility

25. In conducting a disciplinary interview, a supervisor finds that he must ask some highly personal questions which are relevant to the problem at hand. 25.____
The interviewer is MOST likely to get TRUTHFUL answers to these questions if he asks them
A. early in the interview, before the interviewee has had a chance to become emotional
B. in a manner so that the interviewee can answer them with a simple "yes" or "no"
C. well into the interview, after rapport and trust have been established
D. just after the close of the interview, so that the questions appear to be off the record

KEY (CORRECT ANSWERS)

1.	A	11.	A
2.	D	12.	D
3.	D	13.	D
4.	B	14.	A
5.	A	15.	D
6.	D	16.	A
7.	D	17.	B
8.	C	18.	C
9.	B	19.	A
10.	A	20.	A

21.	D
22.	A
23.	B
24.	A
25.	C

TEST 2

DIRECTIONS: Each question or incomplete statement is followed by several suggested answers or completions. Select the one that BEST answers the question or completes the statement. *PRINT THE LETTER OF THE CORRECT ANSWER IN THE SPACE AT THE RIGHT.*

1. Of the following methods of conducting an interview, the BEST is to 1.____
   A. ask questions with "yes" or "no" answers
   B. listen carefully and ask only questions that are pertinent
   C. fire questions at the interviewee so that he must answer sincerely and briefly
   D. read standardized questions to the person being interviewed

2. An interviewer should begin with topics which are easy to talk about and which are not threatening. 2.____
   This procedure is useful MAINLY because it
   A. allows the applicant a little time to get accustomed to the situation and leads to freer communication
   B. distracts the attention of the person being interviewed from the main purpose of the questioning
   C. is the best way for the interviewer to show that he is relaxed and confident on the job
   D. causes the interviewee to feel that the interviewer is apportioning valuable questioning time

3. The initial interview will normally be more of a problem to the interviewer than any subsequent interviews he may have with the same person because 3.____
   A. the interviewee is likely to be hostile
   B. there is too much to be accomplished in one session
   C. he has less information about the client than he will have later
   D. some information may be forgotten when later making record of this first interview

4. Most successful interviews are those in which the interviewer shows a genuine interest in the person he is questioning. 4.____
   This attitude would MOST likely cause the individual being interviewed to
   A. feel that the interviewer already knows all the facts in his case
   B. act more naturally and reveal more of his true feelings
   C. request that the interviewer give more attention to his problems, not his personality
   D. react defensively, suppress his negative feelings and conceal the real facts in his case

5. When interviewing a person, the interviewer may easily slip into error in rating his subject's personal qualities because of the general impression he receives of the individual. 5.____
   This tendency is known as the
   A. "halo" effect
   B. subjective bias problem
   C. "person-to-person" error
   D. inflation effect

6. An interviewer would find an interview checklist LEAST useful for 6.____
   A. making sure that all the principal facts are secured in the interview
   B. insuring that the claimant's grievance is settled in his favor
   C. facilitating later research into the nature of the problems handled by the agency
   D. conducting the interview in a logical and orderly fashion

7. There are almost as many techniques of interviewing as there are interviews. Of the following, the LEAST objectionable method is to 7.____
   A. ask if interviewee minds being quoted
   B. make occasional notes as important topics some up
   C. take notes unobtrusively
   D. take shorthand notes of every word

8. Questions worded so that the person being interviewed has some hint of the desired answer can modify the person's response. 8.____
   The result of the inclusion of such questions in an interview, even when they ae used inadvertently, is to
   A. have no effect on the basic content of the information given by the person interviewed
   B. have value in convincing the person that the suggested plan is the best for him
   C. cause the person to give more meaningful information
   D. reduce the validity of the meaningful information obtained from the person

9. The person MOST likely to be a good interviewer is one who 9.____
   A. is able to outguess the person being interviewed
   B. tries to change the attitudes of the persons he interviews
   C. controls the interview by skillfully dominating the conversation
   D. is able to imagine himself in the position of the person being interviewed

10. The "halo effect" is an overall impression on the interviewee, whether favorable or unfavorable, usually created by a single trait. This impression then influences the appraisal of all other factors. 10.____
    A "halo effect" is LEAST likely to be created at an interview where the interviewee is a
    A. person of average appearance and ability
    B. rough-looking man who uses abusive language
    C. young attractive woman being interviewed by a man
    D. person who demonstrates an exceptional ability to remember faces

11. Of the following, the BEST way for an interviewer to calm a person who seems to have become emotionally upset as a result of a question asked is for the interviewer to 11.____
    A. talk to the person about other things for a short time
    B. ask that the person control himself
    C. probe for the cause of his emotional upset
    D. finish the questioning as quickly as possible

12. Of the following, the GREATEST pitfall in interviewing is that the result may be affected by the 12.____
    A. bias of the interviewee
    B. bias of the interviewer
    C. educational level of the interviewee
    D. educational level of the interviewer

13. Assume you are assigned to interview applicants. 13.____
    Of the following, which is the BEST attitude for you to take in dealing with applicants?
    A. Assume they will enjoy being interviewed because they believe that you have the power of decision
    B. Expect that they have a history of anti-social behavior in the family, and probe deeply into the social development of family members
    C. Expect that they will try to control the interview, thus you should keep them on the defensive
    D. Assume that they will be polite and cooperative and attempt to secure the information you need in a business-like manner

14. A Spanish-speaking applicant may want to bring his bilingual child with him to an interview to act as an interpreter. 14.____
    Which of the following would be LEAST likely to affect the value of an interview in which an applicant's child has acted as interpreter?
    A. It may make it undesirable to ask certain questions.
    B. A child may do an inadequate job of interpretation.
    C. A child's answers may indicate his feelings toward his parents.
    D. The applicant may not want to reveal all information in front of his child.

15. In answering questions asked by students, faculty, and the public, it is MOST important that 15.____
    A. you indicate your source of information
    B. you are not held responsible for the answers
    C. the facts you give be accurate
    D. the answers cover every possible aspect of each question

16. Assume that someone you are interviewing is reluctant to give you certain information. 16.____
    He would probably be MORE responsive if you show him that
    A. all the other persons you interviewed provided you with the information
    B. it would serve his own best interests to give you the information
    C. the information is very important to you
    D. you are business-like and take a no-nonsense approach

17. Taking notes while you are interviewing someone is MOST likely to 17.____
    A. arouse doubts as to your trustworthiness
    B. give the interviewee confidence in your ability
    C. insure that you record the facts you think are important
    D. make the responses of the interviewee unreliable

18. In developing a role-playing situation to be used to train interviewers, the one of the following that it would be MOST important to use as a guide is that the situation 18.____
    A. allow the role player to identify readily with the role he is to play
    B. be free of actual or potential conflict between the role players
    C. can be clearly recognized by the participants as an actual interview situation that has already taken place
    D. should provide a detailed set of specifications for handling the roles to be played

19. Restating a question before the person being interviewed gives an answer to the original question is usually NOT good practice principally because 19.____
    A. the client will think that you don't know your job
    B. it may confuse the client
    C. the interviewer should know exactly what to ask and how to put the question
    D. it reveals the interviewer's insecurity

20. In interviewing a man who has a grievance, it is IMPORTANT that the interviewer 20.____
    A. take note of such physical responses as shifty eyes
    B. use a lie detector, if possible, to ascertain the truth in doubtful situations
    C. allow the complainant to "tell his story"
    D. place the complainant under oath

21. Ideally, the setting for an interview should NOT include 21.____
    A. an informal opening
    B. privacy and comfort
    C. an atmosphere of leisure
    D. a lie detector

22. Which of the following is an example of a "non-directive" interview? 22.____
    A. The subject directs his remarks at someone other than the interviewer.
    B. The subject discusses any topics that seem to be relevant to him.
    C. The subject has not been directed that he need answer any particular questions.
    D. The interview is confined to the facts of the case and is not directed at eliciting personal information.

23. Of the following abilities, the one which is LEAST important in conducting an interview is the ability to 23.____
    A. ask the interviewee pertinent questions
    B. evaluate the interviewee on the basis of appearance
    C. evaluate the responses of the interviewee
    D. gain the cooperation of the interviewee

24. Which of the following actions would be LEAST desirable for you to take when you have to conduct an interview? 24.____
    A. Set a relaxed and friendly atmosphere
    B. Plan your interview ahead of time
    C. Allow the person interviewed to structure the interview as he wishes
    D. Include some stock or standard question which you ask everyone.

25. One of the MOST important techniques for conducting good interviews is 25.____
    A. asking the applicant questions in rapid succession, thereby keeping the conversation properly focused
    B. listening carefully to all that the applicant has to say, making mental notes of possible areas for follow-up
    C. indicating to the applicant the criteria and standards on which you will base your judgment
    D. making sure that you are interrupted about five minutes before you wish to end so that you can keep on schedule

KEY (CORRECT ANSWERS)

1.	B	11.	A
2.	A	12.	B
3.	C	13.	D
4.	B	14.	C
5.	A	15.	C
6.	B	16.	B
7.	C	17.	C
8.	D	18.	A
9.	D	19.	B
10.	A	20.	C

21.	D
22.	B
23.	B
24.	C
25.	B

READING COMPREHENSION
UNDERSTANDING AND INTERPRETING WRITTEN MATERIAL

EXAMINATION SECTION

TEST 1

DIRECTIONS: Each question or incomplete statement is followed by several suggested answers or completions. Select the one that BEST answers the question or completes the statement. *PRINT THE LETTER OF THE CORRECT ANSWER IN THE SPACE AT THE RIGHT.*

Questions 1-5.

DIRECTIONS: Questions 1 through 5 are to be answered SOLELY on the basis of the following passage.

The most effective control mechanism to prevent gross incompetence on the part of public employees is a good personnel program. The personnel officer in the line departments and the central personnel agency should exert positive leadership to raise levels of performance. Although the key factor is the quality of the personnel recruited, staff members other than personnel officers can make important contributions to efficiency. Administrative analysts, now employed in many agencies, make detailed studies of organization and procedures, with the purpose of eliminating delays, waste, and other inefficiencies. Efficiency is, however, more than a question of good organization and procedures; it is also the product of the attitudes and value of the public employees. Personal motivation can provide the will to be efficient. The best management studies will not result in substantial improvement of the performance of those employees who feel no great urge to wok up to their abilities.

1. The above passage indicates that the KEY factor in preventing gross incompetence of public employees is the 1.____
   A. hiring of administrative analysts to assist personnel people
   B. utilization of effective management studies
   C. overlapping of responsibility
   D. quality of the employees hired

2. According to the above passage, the central personnel agency staff SHOULD 2.____
   A. work more closely with administrative analysts in the line departments than with personnel officers
   B. make a serious effort to avoid jurisdictional conflicts with personnel officers in line departments
   C. contribute to improving the quality of work of public employees
   D. engage in a comprehensive program to change the public's negative image of public employees

3. The above passage indicates that efficiency in an organization can BEST be brought about by 3.____
   A. eliminating ineffective control mechanisms
   B. instituting sound organizational procedures
   C. promoting competent personnel
   D. recruiting people with desire to do good work

4. According to the above passage, the purpose of administrative analysts in a public agency is to 4.____
   A. prevent injustice to the public employee
   B. promote the efficiency of the agency
   C. protect the interests of the public
   D. ensure the observance of procedural due process

5. The above passage implies that a considerable rise in the quality of work of public employees can be brought about by 5.____
   A. encouraging positive employee attitudes toward work
   B. controlling personnel officers who exceed their powers
   C. creating warm personal associations among public employees in an agency
   D. closing loopholes in personnel organization and procedures

Questions 6-8.

DIRECTIONS: Questions 6 through 8 are to be answered SOLELY on the basis of the following passage.

EMPLOYEE NEEDS

The greatest waste in industry and in government may be that of human resources. This waste usually derives not from employees' unwillingness or inability, but from management's ineptness to meet the maintenance and motivational needs of employees. Maintenance needs refer to such needs as providing employees with safe places to work, written work rules, job security, adequate salary, employer-sponsored social activities, and with knowledge of their role in the overall framework of the organization. However, of greatest significance to employees are the motivational needs of job growth, achievement, responsibility, and recognition.

Although employee dissatisfaction may stem from either poor maintenance or poor motivation factors, the outward manifestation of the dissatisfaction may be very much like, i.e., negativism, complaints, deterioration of performance, and so forth. The improvement in the lighting of an employee's work area or raising his level of ay won't do much good if the source of the dissatisfaction is the absence of a meaningful assignment. By the same token, if an employee is dissatisfied with what he considers inequitable pay, the introduction of additional challenge in his work may simply make matters worse.

It is relatively easy for an employee to express frustration by complaining about pay, washroom conditions, fringe benefits, and so forth; but most people cannot easily express resentment in terms of the more abstract concepts concerning job growth, responsibility, and achievement.

It would be wrong to assume that there is no interaction between maintenance and motivational needs of employee. For example, conditions of high motivation often overshadow poor maintenance conditions. If an organization is in a period of strong growth and expansion, opportunities for job growth, responsibility, recognition, and achievement are usually abundant, but the rapid growth may have outrun the upkeep of maintenance factors. In this situation, motivation may be high, but only if employees recognize the poor maintenance conditions as unavoidable and temporary. The subordination of maintenance factors cannot go on indefinitely, even with the highest motivation.

Both maintenance and motivation factors influence the behavior of all employees, but employees are not identical and, furthermore, the needs of any individual do not remain orientation toward maintenance factors and those with greater sensitivity toward motivation factors.

A highly maintenance-oriented individual, preoccupied with the factors peripheral to his job rather than the job itself, is more concerned with comfort than challenge. He does not get deeply involved with his work but does with the condition of his work area, toilet facilities, and his time for going to lunch. By contrast, a strongly motivation-oriented employee is usually relatively indifferent to his surroundings and is caught up in the pursuit of work goals.

Fortunately, there are few people who are either exclusively maintenance-oriented or purely motivation-oriented. The former would be deadwood in an organization, while the latter might trample on those around him in his pursuit to achieve his goals.

6. With respect to employee motivational and maintenance needs, the management policies of an organization which is growing rapidly will probably result 6.____
   A. more in meeting motivational needs rather than maintenance needs
   B. more in meeting maintenance needs rather than motivational needs
   C. in meeting both of these needs equally
   D. in increased effort to define the motivational and maintenance needs of its employees

7. In accordance with the above passage, which of the following CANNOT be considered as an example of an employee maintenance need for railroad clerks? 7.____
   A. Providing more relief periods
   B. Providing fair salary increases at periodic intervals
   C. Increasing job responsibilities
   D. Increasing health insurance benefits

8. Most employees in an organization may be categorized as being interested in 8.____
   A. maintenance needs only
   B. motivational needs only
   C. both motivational and maintenance needs
   D. money only, to the exclusion of all other needs

Questions 9-11.

DIRECTIONS: Questions 9 through 11 are to be answered SOLELY on the basis of the following passage.

GOOD EMPLOYEE PRACTICES

As a city employee, you will be expected to take an interest in you work and perform the duties of your job to the best of your ability and in a spirit of cooperation. Nothing shows an interest in your work more than coming to work on time, not only at the start of the day but also when returning from lunch. If it is necessary for you to keep a personal appointment at lunch hour which might cause a delay in getting back to work on time, you should explain the situation to your supervisor and get his approval to come back a little late before you leave for lunch.

You should do everything that is asked of you willingly and consider important even the small jobs that your supervisor gives you. Although these jobs may seem unimportant, if you forget to do them or if you don't do them right, trouble may develop later.

Getting along well with your fellow workers will add much to the enjoyment of your work. You should respect your fellow workers and try to see their side when a disagreement arises. The better you get along with your fellow workers and your supervisor, the better you will like your job and the better you will be able to do it.

9. According to the above passage, in your job as a city employee, you are expected to 9.____
   A. show a willingness to cooperate on the job
   B. get your supervisor's approval before keeping any personal appointments at lunch hour
   C. avoid doing small jobs that seem unimportant
   D. do the easier jobs at the start of the day and the more difficult ones later on

10. According to the above passage, getting to work on time shows that you 10.____
   A. need the job
   B. have an interest in your work
   C. get along well with your fellow workers
   D. like your supervisor

11. According to the above passage, the one of the following statements that is NOT true is: 11.____
   A. If you do a small job wrong, trouble may develop
   B. You should respect your fellow workers
   C. If you disagree with a fellow worker, you should try to see his side of the story
   D. The less you get along with your supervisor, the better you will be able to do your job

Questions 12-15.

DIRECTIONS: Questions 12 through 15 are to be answered SOLELY on the basis of the following passage.

EMPLOYEE SUGGESTIONS

To increase the effectiveness of the city government, the city asks its employees to offer suggestions when they feel an improvement could be made in some government operation. The Employees' Suggestions Program was started to encourage city employees to do this. Through this Program, which is only for city employees, cash awards may be given to those whose suggestions are submitted and approved. Suggestions are looked for not only from supervisors but from all city employees as any city employee may get an idea which might be approved and contribute greatly to the solution of some problem of city government.

Therefore, all suggestions for improvement are welcome, whether they be suggestions on how to improve working conditions, or on how to increase the speed with which work is done, or on how to reduce or eliminate such things as waste, time losses, accidents or fire hazards. There are, however, a few types of suggestions for which cash awards cannot be given. An example of this type would be a suggestion to increase salaries or a suggestion to change the regulations about annual leave or about sick leave. The number of suggestions sent in has increased sharply during the past few years. It is hoped that it will keep increasing in the future in order to meet the city's needs for more ideas for improved ways of doing things.

12. According to the above passage, the MAIN reason why the city asks its employees for suggestions about government operations is to 12.____
    A. increase the effectiveness of the city government
    B. show that the Employees' Suggestion Program is working well
    C. show that everybody helps run the city government
    D. have the employee win a prize

13. According to the above passage, the Employees' Suggestion Program can approve awards ONLY for those suggestions that come from 13.____
    A. city employees
    B. city employees who are supervisors
    C. city employees who are not supervisors
    D. experienced employee of the city

14. According to the above passage, a cash award cannot be given through the Employees' Suggestion Program for a suggestion about 14.____
    A. getting work done faster
    B. helping prevent accidents on the job
    C. increasing the amount of annual leave for city employees
    D. reducing the chance of fire where city employees work

15. According to the above passage, the suggestions sent in during the past few years have 15.____
    A. all been approved
    B. generally been well written
    C. been mostly about reducing or eliminating waste
    D. been greater in number than before

Questions 16-18.

DIRECTIONS: Questions 16 through 18 are to be answered SOLELY on the basis of the following passage.

The supervisor will gain the respect of the members of his staff and increase his influence over them by controlling his temper and avoiding criticizing anyone publicly. When a mistake is made, the good supervisor will take it over with the employee quietly and privately. The supervisor will listen to the employee's story, suggest the better way of doing the job, and offer help so the mistake won't happen again. Before closing the discussion, the supervisor should try to find something good to say about other parts of the employee's work. Some praise and appreciation, along with instruction, is more likely to encourage an employee to improve in those areas where he is weakest.

16. A good title that would show the meaning of the above passage would be 16.____
    A. How to Correct Employee Errors
    B. How to Praise Employees
    C. Mistakes are Preventable
    D. The Weak Employee

17. According to the above passage, the work of an employee who has made a mistake is more likely to improve if the supervisor 17.____
    A. avoids criticizing him
    B. gives him a chance to suggest a better way of doing the work
    C. listens to the employee's excuses to see if he is right
    D. praises good work at the same time he corrects the mistake

18. According to the above passage, when a supervisor needs to correct an employee's mistake, it is important that he 18.____
    A. allow some time to go by after the mistake is made
    B. do so when other employee are not present
    C. show his influence with his tone of voice
    D. tell other employee to avoid the same mistake

Questions 19-23.

DIRECTIONS: Questions 19 through 23 are to be answered SOLELY on the basis of the following passage.

In studying the relationships of people to the organizational structure, it is absolutely necessary to identify and recognize the informal organizational structure. These relationships are necessary when coordination of a plan is attempted. They may be with *the boss*, line supervisors, staff personnel, or other representatives of the formal organization's hierarchy, and they may include the *liaison men* who serve as the leaders of the informal organization. An acquaintanceship with the people serving in these roles in the organization, and its formal counterpart, permits a supervisor to recognize sensitive areas in which it is simple to get conflict reaction. Avoidance of such areas, plus conscious efforts to inform other people of his own objectives for various plans, will usually enlist their aid and support. Planning *without* people can lead to disaster because the individuals who must act together to make any plan a success are more important than the plans themselves.

19. Of the following titles, the one that MOST clearly describes the above passage is 19.____
    A. Coordination of a Function
    B. Avoidance of Conflict
    C. Planning With People
    D. Planning Objectives

20. According to the above passage, attempts at coordinating plans may fail unless 20.____
    A. the plan's objectives are clearly set forth
    B. conflict between groups is resolved
    C. the plans themselves are worthwhile
    D. informal relationships are recognized

21. According to the above passage, conflict 21.____
    A. may, in some cases, be desirable to secure results
    B. produces more heat than light
    C. should be avoided at all costs
    D. possibilities can be predicted by a sensitive supervisor

22. The above passage implies that 22.____
    A. informal relationships are more important than formal structure
    B. the weakness of a formal structure depends upon informal relationships
    C. liaison men are the key people to consult when taking formal and informal structures into account
    D. individuals in a group are at least as important as the plans for the group

23. The above passage suggests that 23.____
    A. some planning can be disastrous
    B. certain people in sensitive areas should be avoided
    C. the supervisor should discourage acquaintanceships in the organization
    D. organizational relationships should be consciously limited

Questions 24-25.

DIRECTIONS: Questions 24 and 25 are to be answered SOLELY on the basis of the following passage.

Good personnel relations of an organization depend upon mutual confidence, trust, and good will. The basis of confidence is understanding. Most troubles start with people who do not understand each other. When the organization's intentions or motives are misunderstood, or when reasons for actions, practices, or policies are misconstrued, complete cooperation from individuals is not forthcoming. If management expects full cooperation from employees, it has a responsibility of sharing with them the information which is the foundation of proper understanding, confidence, and trust. Personnel management has long since outgrown the days when it was the vogue to *treat them rough and tell them nothing.* Up-to-date personnel management provides all possible information about the activities, aims, and purposes of the organization. It seems altogether creditable that a desire should exist among employees for such information which the best-intentioned executive might think would not interest them and which the worst-intentioned would think was none of their business.

24. The above passage implies that one of the causes of the difficulty which an organization might have with its personnel relations is that its employees 24.____
    A. have not expressed interest in the activities, aims, and purposes of the organization
    B. do not believe in the good faith of the organization
    C. have not been able to give full cooperation to the organization
    D. do not recommend improvements in the practices and policies of the organization

25. According to the above passage, in order for an organization to have good personnel relations, it is NOT essential that 25.____
    A. employees have confidence in the organization
    B. the purposes of the organization be understood by the employees
    C. employees have a desire for information about the organization
    D. information about the organization be communicated to employees

KEY (CORRECT ANSWERS)

1.	D	11.	D
2.	C	12.	A
3.	D	13.	A
4.	B	14.	C
5.	A	15.	D
6.	A	16.	A
7.	C	17.	D
8.	C	18.	B
9.	A	19.	C
10.	B	20.	D

21.	D
22.	D
23.	A
24.	B
25.	C

TEST 2

DIRECTIONS: Each question or incomplete statement is followed by several suggested answers or completions. Select the one that BEST answers the question or completes the statement. *PRINT THE LETTER OF THE CORRECT ANSWER IN THE SPACE AT THE RIGHT.*

Questions 1-8.

DIRECTIONS: Questions 1 through 8 are to be answered SOLELY on the basis of the following passage.

Important figures in education and in public affairs have recommended development of a private organization sponsored in part by various private foundations which would offer installment payment plans to full-time matriculated students in accredited colleges and universities in the United States and Canada. Contracts would be drawn to cover either tuition and fees, or tuition, fees, room and board in college facilities, from one year up to and including six years. A special charge, which would vary with the length of the contract, would be added to the gross repayable amount. This would be in addition to interest at a rate which would vary with the income of the parents. There would be a 3% annual interest charge for families with total income, before income taxes, of $50,000 or less. The rate would increase by 1/10 of 1% for every $1,000 of additional net income in excess of $50,000 up to a maximum of 10% interest. Contracts would carry an insurance provision on the life of the parent or guardian who signs the contract; all contracts must have the signature of a parent or guardian. Payment would be scheduled in equal monthly installments.

1. Which of the following students would be eligible for the payment plan described in the above passage? A 1.____
   A. matriculated student taking six semester hours toward a graduate degree
   B. matriculated student taking seventeen semester hours toward an undergraduate degree
   C. graduate matriculated at the University of Mexico taking eighteen semester hours toward a graduate degree
   D. student taking eighteen semester hours in a special pre-matriculation program

2. According to the above passage, the organization described would be sponsored in part by 2.____
   A. private foundations
   B. colleges and universities
   C. persons in the field of education
   D. persons in public life

3. Which of the following expenses could NOT be covered by a contract with the organization described in the above passage? 3.____
   A. Tuition amounting to $20,000 per year
   B. Registration and laboratory fees
   C. Meals at restaurants near the college
   D. Rent for an apartment in a college dormitory

4. The total amount to be paid would include ONLY the 4.____
   A. principal
   B. principal and interest
   C. principal, interest, and special charge
   D. principal, interest, special charge, and fee

5. The contract would carry insurance on the 5.____
   A. life of the student
   B. life of the student's parents
   C. income of the parents of the student
   D. life of the parent who signed the contract

6. The interest rate for an annual loan of $25,000 from the organization described in the above passage for a student whose family's net income was $55,000 should be 6.____
   A. 3% B. 3.5% C. 4% D. 4.5%

7. The interest rate for an annual loan of $35,000 from the organization described in the above passage for a student whose family's net income was $100,000 should be 7.____
   A. 5% B. 8% C. 9% D. 10%

8. John Lee has submitted an application for the installment payment plan described in the above passage. John's mother and father have a store which grossed $500,000 last year, but the income which the family received from the store was $90,000 before taxes. They also had $5,000 income from stock dividends. They paid $10,000 in income taxes. 8.____
   The amount of income upon which the interest should be based is
   A. $85,000 B. $90,000 C. $95,000 D. $105,000

Questions 9-13.

DIRECTIONS: Questions 9 through 13 are to be answered SOLELY on the basis of the following passage.

Since the organization chart is pictorial in nature, there is a tendency for it to be drawn in an artistically balanced and appealing fashion, regardless of the realities of actual organizational structure. In addition to being subject to this distortion, there is the difficulty of communicating in any organization chart the relative importance or the relative size of various component parts of an organizational structure. Furthermore, because of the need for simplicity of design, an organization chart can never indicate the full extent of the interrelationships among the component parts of an organization.

These interrelationships are often just as vital as the specifications which an organization chart endeavors to indicate. Yet, if an organization chart were to be drawn with all the wide variety of criss-crossing communication and cooperation networks existent within a typical organization, the chart would probably be much more confusing than informative. It is also obvious that no organization chart as such can prove or disprove that the organizational structure it represents is effective in realizing the objectives of the organization. At best, an organization chart can only illustrate some of the various factors to be taken into consideration in understanding, devising, or altering organizational arrangements.

9. According to the above passage, an organization chart can be expected to portray the 9.____
   A. structure of the organization along somewhat ideal lines
   B. relative size of the organizational units quite accurately
   C. channels of information distribution within the organization graphically
   D. extent of the obligation of each unit to meet the organizational objectives

10. According to the above passage, those aspects of internal functioning which are NOT shown on an organization chart 10.____
   A. can be considered to have little practical application in the operations of the organization
   B. might well be considered to be as important as the structural relationships which a chart does present
   C. could be the cause of considerable confusion in the operations of an organization which is quite large
   D. would be most likely to provide the information needed to determine the overall effectiveness of an organization

11. In the above passage, the one of the following conditions which is NOT implied as being a defect of an organization chart is that an organization chart may 11.____
   A. present a picture of the organizational structure which is different from the structure that actually exists
   B. fail to indicate the comparative size of various organizational units
   C. be limited in its ability to convey some of the meaningful aspects of organizational relationships
   D. become less useful over a period of time during which the organizational facts which it illustrated have changed

12. The one of the following which is the MOST suitable title for the above passage is 12.____
   A. The Design and Construction of an Organization Chart
   B. The Informal Aspects of an Organization Chart
   C. The Inherent Deficiencies of an Organization Chart
   D. The Utilization of a Typical Organization Chart

13. It can be inferred from the above passage that the function of an organization chart is to 13.____
   A. contribute to the comprehension of the organization form and arrangements
   B. establish the capabilities of the organization to operate effectively
   C. provide a balanced picture of the operations of the organization
   D. eliminate the need for complexity in the organization's structure

Questions 14-16.

DIRECTIONS: Questions 14 through 16 are to be answered SOLELY on the basis of the following passage.

In dealing with visitors to the school office, the school secretary must use initiative, tact, and good judgment. All visitors should be greeted promptly and courteously. The nature of their business should be determined quickly and handled expeditiously. Frequently, the secretary should be able to handle requests, deliveries, or passes herself. Her judgment should determine when a visitor should see members of the staff or the principal. Serious problems or doubtful cases should be referred to a supervisor.

14. In general, visitors should be handled by the 14.____
   A. school secretary
   B. principal
   C. appropriate supervisor
   D. person who is free

15. It is wise to obtain the following information from visitors: 15.____
   A. Name
   B. Nature of business
   C. Address
   D. Problems they have

16. All visitors who wish to see members of the staff should 16.____
   A. be permitted to do so
   B. produce identification
   C. do so for valid reasons only
   D. be processed by a supervisor

Questions 17-19.

DIRECTIONS: Questions 17 through 19 are to be answered SOLELY on the basis of the following passage.

Information regarding payroll status, salary differentials, promotional salary increments, deductions, and pension payments should be given to all members of the staff who have questions regarding these items. On occasion, if the secretary is uncertain regarding the information, the staff member should be referred to the principal or the appropriate agency. No question by a staff member regarding payroll status should be brushed aside as immaterial or irrelevant. The school secretary must always try to handle the question or pass it on to the person who can handle it.

17. If a teacher is dissatisfied with information regarding her salary status, as given by the school secretary, the matter should be 17.____
   A. dropped
   B. passed on to the principal
   C. passed on by the secretary to proper agency or the principal
   D. made a basis for grievance procedures

18. The following is an adequate summary of the above passage: 18.____
   A. The secretary must handle all payroll matters
   B. The secretary must handle all payroll matter or know who can handle them
   C. The secretary or the principal must handle all payroll matters
   D. Payroll matter too difficult to handle must be followed up until they are solved

19. The above passage implies that 19.____
    A. many teachers ask immaterial questions regarding payroll status
    B. few teachers ask irrelevant pension questions
    C. no teachers ask immaterial salary questions
    D. no question regarding salary should be considered irrelevant

Questions 20-22.

DIRECTIONS: Questions 20 through 22 are to be answered SOLELY on the basis of the following passage.

The necessity for good speech on the part of the school secretary cannot be overstated. The school secretary must deal with the general public, the pupils, the members of the staff, and the school supervisors. In every situation which involves the general public, the secretary serves as a representative of the school. In dealing with pupils, the secretary's speech must serve as a model from which students may guide themselves. Slang, colloquialisms, malapropisms, and local dialects must be avoided.

20. The above passage implies that the speech pattern of the secretary must be 20.____
    A. perfect
    B. very good
    C. average
    D. on a level with that of the pupils

21. The last sentence indicates that slang 21.____
    A. is acceptable
    B. occurs in all speech
    C. might be used occasionally
    D. should be shunned

22. The above passage implies that the speech of pupils 22.____
    A. may be influenced
    B. does not change readily
    C. is generally good
    D. is generally poor

Questions 23-25.

DIRECTIONS: Questions 23 through 25 are to be answered SOLELY on the basis of the following passage.

The school secretary who is engaged in the task of filing records and correspondence should follow a general set of rules. Items which are filed should be available to other secretaries or to supervisors quickly and easily by means of the application of a modicum of common sense and good judgment. Items which, by their nature, may be difficult to find should be cross-indexed. Folders and drawers should be neatly and accurately labeled. There should never be a large accumulation of papers which have not been filed.

23. A good general rule to follow in filing is that materials should be 23.____
    A. placed in folders quickly
    B. neatly stored
    C. readily available
    D. cross-indexed

24. Items that are filed should be available to 24.____
    A. the secretary charged with the task of filing
    B. secretaries and supervisors
    C. school personnel
    D. the principal

25. A modicum of common sense means _____ common sense. 25.____
    A. an average amount of
    B. a great deal of
    C. a little
    D. no

KEY (CORRECT ANSWERS)

1.	B	11.	D
2.	A	12.	C
3.	C	13.	A
4.	C	14.	A
5.	D	15.	B
6.	B	16.	C
7.	B	17.	C
8.	C	18.	B
9.	A	19.	D
10.	B	20.	B

21.	D
22.	A
23.	C
24.	B
25.	C

TEST 3

DIRECTIONS: Each question or incomplete statement is followed by several suggested answers or completions. Select the one that BEST answers the question or completes the statement. *PRINT THE LETTER OF THE CORRECT ANSWER IN THE SPACE AT THE RIGHT.*

Questions 1-4.

DIRECTIONS: Questions 1 through 4 are to be answered SOLELY on the basis of the following passage.

The proposition that administrative activity is essentially the same in all organizations appears to underlie some of the practices in the administration of private higher education. Although the practice is unusual in public education, there are numerous instances of industrial, governmental, or military administrators being assigned to private institutions of higher education and, to a lesser extent, of college and university presidents assuming administrative positions in other types of organizations. To test this theory that administrators are interchangeable, there is a need for systematic observation and classification. The myth that an educational administrator must first have experience in the teaching profession is firmly rooted in a long tradition that has historical prestige. The myth is bound up in the expectations of the public and personnel surrounding the administrator. Since administrative success depends significantly on how well an administrator meets the expectations others have of him, the myth may be more powerful than the special experience in helping the administrator attain organizational and educational objectives. Educational administrators who have risen through the teaching profession have often expressed nostalgia for the life of a teacher or scholar, but there is no evidence that this nostalgia contributes to administrative success.

1. Which of the following statements as completed is MOST consistent with the above passage? 1.____
The greatest number of administrators has moved from
   A. industry and the military to government and universities
   B. government and universities to industry and the military
   C. government, the armed forces, and industry to colleges and universities
   D. colleges and universities to government, the armed forces, and industry

2. Of the following, the MOST reasonable inference from the above passage is that a specific area requiring further research is the 2.____
   A. place of myth in the tradition and history of the educational profession
   B. relative effectiveness of educational administrators from inside and outside the teaching profession
   C. performance of administrators in the administration of public colleges
   D. degree of reality behind the nostalgia for scholarly pursuits often expressed by educational administrators

3. According to the above passage, the value to an educational administrator of experience in the teaching profession 3.____
   A. lies in the first-hand knowledge he has acquired of immediate educational problems
   B. may lie in the belief of his colleagues, subordinates, and the public that such experience is necessary
   C. has been supported by evidence that the experience contributes to administrative success in educational fields
   D. would be greater if the administrator were able to free himself from nostalgia for his former duties

4. Of the following, the MOST suitable title for the above passage is 4.____
   A. Educational Administration, Its Problems
   B. The Experience Needed For Educational Administration
   C. Administration in Higher Education
   D. Evaluating Administrative Experience

Questions 5-6.

DIRECTIONS: Questions 5 and 6 are to be answered SOLELY on the basis of the following passage.

Management by objectives (MBO) may be defined as the process by which the superior and the subordinate managers of an organization jointly define its common goals, define each individual's major areas of responsibility in terms of the results expected of him and use these measure as guides for operating the unit and assessing the contribution of each of its members.

The MBO approach requires that after organizational goals are established and communicated, targets must be set for each individual position which are congruent with organizational goals. Periodic performance reviews and a final review using the objectives set as criteria are also basic to this approach.

Recent studies have shown that MBO programs are influenced by attitudes and perceptions of the boss, the company, the reward-punishment system, and the program itself. In addition, the manner in which the MBO program is carried out can influence the success of the program. A study done in the late sixties indicates that the best results are obtained when the manager sets goals which deal with significant problem areas in the organizational unit, or with the subordinate's personal deficiencies. These goals must be clear with regard to what is expected of the subordinate. The frequency of feedback is also important in the success of a management-by-objectives program. Generally, the greater the amount of feedback, the more successful the MBO program.

5. According to the above passage, the expected output for individual employees should be determined 5.____
   A. after a number of reviews of work performance
   B. after common organizational goals are defined
   C. before common organizational goals are defined
   D. on the basis of an employee's personal qualities

6. According to the above passage, the management-by-objectives approach requires 6.____
   A. less feedback than other types of management programs
   B. little review of on-the-job performance after the initial setting of goals
   C. general conformance between individual goals and organizational goals
   D. the setting of goals which deal with minor problem areas in the organization

Questions 7-10.

DIRECTIONS: Questions 7 through 10 are to be answered SOLELY on the basis of the following passage.

Management, which is the function of executive leadership, has as its principal phases the planning, organizing, and controlling of the activities of subordinate groups in the accomplishment of organizational objectives. Planning specifies the kind and extent of the factors, forces, and effects, and the relationships among them, that will be required for satisfactory accomplishment. The nature of the objectives and their requirements must be known before determinations can be made as to what must be done, how it must be done and why, where actions should take place, who should be responsible, and similar programs pertaining to the formulation of a plan. Organizing, which creates the conditions that must be present before the execution of the plan can be undertaken successfully, cannot be done intelligently without knowledge of the organizational objectives. Control, which has to do with the constraint and regulation of activities entering into the execution of the plan, must be exercised in accordance with the characteristics and requirements of the activities demanded by the plan.

7. The one of the following which is the MOST suitable title for the above passage is 7.____
   A. The Nature of Successful Organization
   B. The Planning of Management Functions
   C. The Importance of Organizational Functions
   D. The Principle Aspects of Management

8. It can be inferred from the above passage that the one of the following functions whose existence is essential to the existence of the other three is the 8.____
   A. regulation of the work needed to carry out a plan
   B. understanding of what the organization intends to accomplish
   C. securing of information of the factors necessary for accomplishment of objectives
   D. establishment of the conditions required for successful action

9. The one of the following which would NOT be included within any of the principal phases of the function of executive leadership as defined in the above passage is 9.____
   A. determination of manpower requirements
   B. procurement of required material
   C. establishment of organizational objectives
   D. scheduling of production

10. The conclusion which can MOST reasonably be drawn from the above passage is that the control phase of managing is most directly concerned with the 10.____
    A. influencing of policy determinations
    B. administering of suggestion systems
    C. acquisition of staff for the organization
    D. implementation of performance standards

Questions 11-12.

DIRECTIONS: Questions 11 and 12 are to be answered SOLELY on the basis of the following passage.

Under an open-and-above-board policy, it is to be expected that some supervisors will gloss over known shortcomings of subordinates rather than face the task of discussing team face-to-face. It is also to be expected that at least some employees whose job performance is below par will reject the supervisor's appraisal as biased and unfair. Be that as it may, these are inescapable aspects of any performance appraisal system in which human beings are involved. The supervisor who shies away from calling a spade a spade, as well as the employee with a chip on his shoulder, will each in his own way eventually be revealed in his true light—to the benefit of the organization as a whole.

11. The BEST of the following interpretations of the above passage is that 11.____
    A. the method of rating employee performance requires immediate revision to improve employee acceptance
    B. substandard performance ratings should be discussed with employees even if satisfactory ratings are not
    C. supervisors run the risk of being called unfair by the subordinates even though their appraisals are accurate
    D. any system of employee performance rating is satisfactory if used properly

12. The BEST of the following interpretations of the above passage is that 12.____
    A. supervisors generally are not open-and-above-board with their subordinates
    B. it is necessary for supervisors to tell employees objectively how they are performing
    C. employees complain when their supervisor does not keep them informed
    D. supervisors are afraid to tell subordinates their weaknesses

Questions 13-15.

DIRECTIONS: Questions 13 through 15 are to be answered SOLELY on the basis of the following passage.

During the last decade, a great deal of interest has been generated around the phenomenon of *organizational development,* or the process of developing human resources through conscious organization effort. Organizational development (OD) stresses improving interpersonal relationships and organizational skills, such as communication, to a much greater degree than individual training ever did. The kind of training that an organization should emphasize depends upon the present and future structure of the organization. If future organizations are to be unstable, shifting coalitions, then individual skills and abilities, particularly those emphasizing innovativeness, creativity, flexibility, and the latest technological knowledge, are crucial and individual training is most appropriate.

But if there is to be little change in organizational structure, then the main thrust of training should be group-oriented or organizational development. This approach seems better designed for overcoming hierarchical barriers, for developing a degree of interpersonal relationships which make communication along the chain of command possible, and for retaining a modicum of innovation and/or flexibility.

13. According to the above passage, group-oriented training is MOST useful in in 13.____
   A. developing a communications system that will facilitate understanding through the chain of command
   B. highly flexible and mobile organizations
   C. preventing the crossing of hierarchical barriers within an organization
   D. saving energy otherwise wasted on developing methods of dealing with rigid hierarchies

14. The one of the following conclusions which can be drawn MOST appropriately from the above passage is that 14.____
   A. behavioral research supports the use of organizational development training methods rather than individualized training
   B. it is easier to provide individualized training in specific skills than to set up sensitivity training programs
   C. organizational development eliminates innovative or flexible activity
   D. the nature of an organization greatly influences which training methods will be most effective

15. According to the above passage, the one of the following which is LEAST important for large-scale organizations geared to rapid and abrupt change is 15.____
   A. current technological information
   B. development of a high degree of interpersonal relationships
   C. development of individual skills and abilities
   D. emphasis on creativity

Questions 16-18.

DIRECTIONS: Questions 16 through 18 are to be answered SOLELY on the basis of the following passage.

The increase in the extent to which each individual is personally responsible to others is most noticeable in a large bureaucracy. No one person *decides* anything; each decision of any importance, is the product of an intricate process of brokerage involving individuals inside and outside the organization who feel some reason to be affected by the decision, or two have special knowledge to contribute to it. The more varied the organization's constituency, the more inside *veto-groups* will need to be taken into account. But even if no outside consultations were involved, sheer size would produce a complex process of decision. For a large organization is a deliberately created system of tensions into which each individual is expected to bring work-ways, viewpoints, and outside relationships markedly different from those of his colleagues. It is the administrator's task to draw from these disparate forces the elements of wise action from day to day, consistent with the purposes of the organization as a whole.

16. The above passage is essentially a description of decision-making as 16.____
    A. an organization process
    B. the key responsibility of the administrator
    C. the one best position among many
    D. a complex of individual decisions

17. Which one of the following statements BEST describes the responsibilities of an administrator? 17.____
    A. He modifies decisions and goals in accordance with pressures from within and outside the organization.
    B. He creates problem-solving mechanisms that rely on the varied interests of his staff and *veto-groups*.
    C. He makes determinations that will lead to attainment of his agency's objectives.
    D. He obtains agreement among varying viewpoints and interests

18. In the context of the operations of a central public personnel agency, a *veto-group* would LEAST likely consist of 18.____
    A. employee organizations
    B. professional personnel societies
    C. using agencies
    D. civil service newspapers

Questions 19-25.

DIRECTIONS: Questions 19 through 25 are to be answered SOLELY on the basis of the following passage, which is an extract from a report prepared for Department X, which outlines the procedure to be followed in the case of transfers of employees.

Every transfer, regardless of the reason therefore, requires completion of the record of transfer, Form DT411. To denote consent to the transfer, DT411 should contain the signatures of the transferee and the personnel officer(s) concerned, except that, in the case of an involuntary transfer, the signatures of the transferee's present and prospective supervisors shall be entered in Boxes 8A and 8B, respectively, since the transferee does not consent. Only a permanent employee may request a transfer; in such cases, the employee's attendance record shall be duly considered with regard to absences, latenesses, and accrued overtime balances. In the case of an inter-district transfer, the employee's attendance record must be included in Section 8A of the transfer request, Form DT410, by the personnel officer of the district from which the transfer is requested. The personnel officer of the district to which the employee requested transfer may refuse to accept accrued overtime balances in excess of ten days.

An employee on probation shall be eligible for transfer. If such employee is involuntarily transferred, he shall be credited for the period of time already served on probation. However, if such transfer is voluntary, the employee shall be required to serve the entire period of his probation in the new position. An employee who has occurred a disability which prevents him from performing his normal duties may be transferred during the period of such disability to other appropriate duties. A disability transfer requires the completion of either DT414 if the disability is job-connected, or Form DT415 if it is not a job-connected disability. In either case, the personnel officer of the district from which the transfer is made signs in Box 6A of the first two copies and the personnel officer of the district to which the transfer is made signs in Box 6B of the last two copies, or, in the case of an intra-district disability transfer, the personnel officer must sign in Box 6A of the first two copies and Box 6B of the last two copies.

19. When a personnel officer consents to an employee's request for transfer from his district, this procedure requires that the personnel officer sign Forms 19.____
   A. DT411
   B. DT410 and DT411
   C. DT411 and either Form DT414 or DT415
   D. DT410 and DT411, and either Form DT414 or DT415

20. With respect to the time record of an employee transferred against his wishes during his probationary period, this procedure requires that 20.____
   A. he serve the entire period of his probation in his present office
   B. he lose his accrued overtime balance
   C. his attendance record be considered with regard to absences and latenesses
   D. he be given credit for the period of time he has already served on probation

21. Assume you are a supervisor and an employee must be transferred into your office against his wishes. 21.____
   According to this procedure, the box you must sign on the record of transfer is
   A. 6A B. 8A C. 6B D. 8B

22. Under this procedure, in the case of a disability transfer, when must Box 6A on Forms DT414 and DT415 be signed by the personnel officer of the district to which the transfer is being made? 22.____
   A. In all cases when either Form DT414 or Form DT415 is used
   B. In all cases when Form DT414 is used and only under certain circumstances when Form DT415 is used
   C. In all cases when Form DT415 is used and only under certain circumstances when Form DT414 is used
   D. Only under certain circumstances when either Form DT414 or Form DT415 is used

23. From the above passage, it may be inferred MOST correctly that the number of copies of Form DT414 is 23.____
    A. no more than 2
    B. at least 3
    C. at least 5
    D. more than the number of copies of Form DT415

24. A change in punctuation and capitalization only which would change one sentence into two and possibly contribute to somewhat greater ease of reading this report extract would be MOST appropriate in the 24.____
    A. 2nd sentence, 1st paragraph
    B. 3rd sentence, 1st paragraph
    C. next to the last sentence, 2nd paragraph
    D. 2nd sentence, 2nd paragraph

25. In the second paragraph, a word that is INCORRECTLY used is 25.____
    A. *shall* in the 1st sentence
    B. *voluntary* in the 3rd sentence
    C. *occurred* in the 4th sentence
    D. *intra-district* in the last sentence

KEY (CORRECT ANSWERS)

1.	C	11.	C
2.	B	12.	B
3.	B	13.	A
4.	B	14.	D
5.	B	15.	B
6.	C	16.	A
7.	D	17.	C
8.	B	18.	B
9.	C	19.	A
10.	D	20.	D

21.	D
22.	D
23.	B
24.	B
25.	C

PREPARING WRITTEN MATERIAL

PARAGRAPH REARRANGEMENT COMMENTARY

The sentences that follow are in scrambled order. You are to rearrange them in proper order and indicate the letter choice containing the correct answer at the space at the right.

Each group of sentences in this section is actually a paragraph presented in scrambled order. Each sentence in the group has a place in that paragraph; no sentence is to be left out. You are to read each group of sentences and decide upon the best order in which to put the sentences so as to form a well-organized paragraph.

The questions in this section measure the ability to solve a problem when all the facts relevant to its solution are not given.

More specifically, certain positions of responsibility and authority require the employee to discover connection between events sometimes, apparently, unrelated. In order to do this, the employee will find it necessary to correctly infer that unspecified events have probably occurred or are likely to occur. This ability becomes especially important when action must be taken on incomplete information.

Accordingly, these questions require competitors to choose among several suggested alternatives, each of which presents a different sequential arrangement of the events. Competitors must choose the MOST logical of the suggested sequences.

In order to do so, they may be required to draw on general knowledge to infer missing concepts or events that are essential to sequencing the given events. Competitors should be careful to infer only what is essential to the sequence. The plausibility of the wrong alternatives will always require the inclusion of unlikely events or of additional chains of events which are NOT essential to sequencing the given events.

It's very important to remember that you are looking for the best of the four possible choices, and that the best choice of all may not even be one of the answers you're given to choose from.

There is no one right way to solve these problems. Many people have found it helpful to first write out the order of the sentences, as they would have arranged them, on their scrap paper before looking at the possible answers. If their optimum answer is there, this can save them some time. If it isn't, this method can still give insight into solving the problem. Others find it most helpful to just go through each of the possible choices, contrasting each as they go along. You should use whatever method feels comfortable and works for you.

While most of these types of questions are not that difficult, we've added a higher percentage of the difficult type, just to give you more practice. Usually there are only one or two questions on this section that contain such subtle distinctions that you're unable to answer confidently. And you then may find yourself stuck deciding between two possible choices, neither of which you're sure about.

EXAMINATION SECTION

TEST 1

DIRECTIONS: The sentences listed below are part of a meaningful paragraph, but they are not given in their proper order. You are to decide what would be the BEST order to put sentences to form a well-organized paragraph. Each sentence has a place in the paragraph; there are no extra sentences. *PRINT THE LETTER OF THE CORRECT ANSWER IN THE SPACE AT THE RIGHT.*

1. I. He came on a winter's eve. 1.____
   II. Akira came directly, breaking all tradition.
   III. He pounded on the door while a cold rain beat on the shuttered veranda, so at first Chie thought him only the wind.
   IV. Was that it?
   V. Had he followed form—had he asked his mother to speak to his father to approach a go-between—would Chie have been more receptive?

   The CORRECT answer is:
   A. II, IV, V, I, III B. I, III, II, IV, V C. V, IV, II, III, I D. III, V, I, II, IV

2. I. We have an understanding. 2.____
   II. Either method comes down to the same thing: a matter of parental approval.
   III. If you give your consent, I become Naomi's husband.
   IV. Please don't judge my candidacy by the unseemliness of this proposal.
   V. I ask directly because the use of a go-between takes much time.

   The CORRECT answer is:
   A. III, IV, II, V, I B. I, V, II, III, IV C. I, IV, V, II, III D. V, III, I, IV, II

3. I. Many relish the opportunity to buy presents because gift-giving offers a powerful means to build stronger bonds with one's closest peers. 3.____
   II. Aside from purchasing holiday gifts, most people regularly buy presents for other occasions throughout the year, including weddings, birthdays, anniversaries, graduations, and baby showers.
   III. Last year, Americans spent over $30 billion at retail stores in the month of December alone.
   IV. This frequent experience of gift-giving can engender ambivalent feelings in gift-givers.
   V. Every day, millions of shoppers hit the stores in full force—both online and on foot—searching frantically for the perfect gift.

   The CORRECT answer is:
   A. II, III, V, I, IV B. IV, V, I, III, II C. III, II, V, I, IV D. V, III, II, IV, I

4. I. Why do gift-givers assume that gift price is closely linked to gift-recipients' feelings of appreciation? 4.____
II. Perhaps givers believe that bigger (i.e., more expensive) gifts convey stronger signals of thoughtfulness and consideration.
III. In this sense, gift-givers may be motivated to spend more money on a gift in order to send a "stronger signal" to their intended recipient.
IV. According to Camerer (1988) and others, gift-giving represents a symbolic ritual, whereby gift-givers attempt to signal their positive attitudes toward the intended recipient and their willingness to invest resources in a future relationship.
V. As for gift-recipients, they may not construe smaller and larger gifts as representing smaller and larger signals of thoughtfulness and consideration.
The CORRECT answer is:
A. V, III, II, IV, I B. I, II, IV, III, V C. IV, I, III, V, II D. II, V, I, IV, III

5. I. But when the spider is not hungry, the stimulation of its hairs merely causes it to shake the touched limb. 5.____
II. Touching this body hair produces one of two distinct reactions.
III. The entire body of a tarantula, especially its legs, is thickly clothed with hair.
IV. Some of it is short and wooly, some long and stiff.
V. When the spider is hungry, it responds with an immediate and swift attack.
The CORRECT answer is:
A. IV, II, I, III, V B. V, I, III, IV, II C. III, IV, II, V, I D. I, II, IV, III, V

6. I. That tough question may be just one question away from an easy one. 6.____
II. They tend to be arranged sequentially: questions on the first paragraph come before questions on the second paragraph.
III. In summation, it is important not to forget that there is no penalty for guessing.
IV. Try *all* questions on the passage.
V. Remember, the critical reading questions after each passage are not arranged in order of difficulty.
The CORRECT answer is:
A. I, III, IV, II, V B. II, I, V, III, IV C. III, IV, I, V, II D. V, II, IV, I, III

7. I. This time of year clients come to me with one goal in mind: losing weight. 7.____
II. I usually tell them that their goal should be focused on fat loss instead of weight loss.
III. Converting and burning fat while maintaining or building muscle is an art, which also happens to be my job.
IV. What I love about this line of work is that *everyone* benefits from healthy eating and supplemental nutrition.
V. This is because most of us have more stored fat than we prefer, but we do not want to lose muscle in addition to the fat.
The CORRECT answer is:
A. V, III, I, II, IV B. I, IV, V, III, IV C. II, I, III, IV, V D. II, V, IV, I, II

8. I. In Tierra del Fuego, "invasive" describes the beaver perfectly. 8.____
II. What started as a small influx of 50 beavers has since grown to a number over 200,000.
III. Unlike in North America where the beaver has several natural predators that help to maintain manageable population numbers, Tierra del Fuego has no such luxury.
IV. An invasive species is a non-indigenous animal, fungus, or plant species introduced to an area that has the potential to inflict harm upon the native ecosystem.
V. It was first introduced in 1946 by the Argentine government in an effort to catalyze a fur trading industry in the region.
The CORRECT answer is:
A. IV, I, V, II, III B. I, IV, II, III, V C. II, V, III, I, IV D. V, II, IV, III, I

9. I. The words ensure that we are all part of something much larger than the here and now. 9.____
II. Literature might be thought of as the creative measure of history.
III. It seems impossible to disconnect most literary works from their historical context.
IV. Great writers, poets, and playwrights mold their sense of life and the events of their time into works of art.
V. However, the themes that make their work universal and enduring perhaps do transcend time.
The CORRECT answer is:
A. I, III, II, V, IV B. IV, I, V, II, III C. II, IV, III, V, I D. III, V, I, IV, II

10. I. If you don't already have an exercise routine, try to build up to a good 20- to 45-minute aerobic workout. 10.____
II. When your brain is well oxygenated, it works more efficiently, so you do your work better and faster.
III. Your routine will help you enormously when you sit down to work on homework or even on the day of a test.
IV. Twenty minutes of cardiovascular exercise is a great warm-up before you start your homework.
V. Exercise does not just help your muscles; it also helps your brain.
The CORRECT answer is:
A. I, IV, II, IV, III B. IV, V, II, I, III C. V, III, IV, II, I D. III, IV, I, V, II

11. I. Experts often suggest that crime resembles an epidemic, but what kind? 11.____
II. If it travels along major transportation routes, the cause is microbial.
III. Economics professor Karl Smith has a good rule of thumb for categorizing epidemics: if it is along the lines of communication, he says the cause is information.
IV. However, if it spreads everywhere all at once, the cause is a molecule.
V. If it spreads out like a fan, the cause is an insect.
The CORRECT answer is:
A. I, III, II, V, IV B. II, I, V, IV, III C. V, III, I, II, IV D. IV, V, I, III, II

12. I. A recent study had also suggested a link between childhood lead exposure and juvenile delinquency later on. 12.____
II. These ideas all caused Nevin to look into other sources of lead-based items as well, such as gasoline.
III. In 1994, Rick Nevin was a consultant working for the U.S Department of Housing and Urban Development on the costs and benefits of removing lead paint from old houses.
IV. Maybe reducing lead exposure could have an effect on violent crime too?
V. A growing body of research had linked lead exposure in small children with a whole raft of complications later in life, including lower IQ and behavioral problems.
The CORRECT answer is:
A. I, III, V, II, IV B. IV, I, II, V, III C. I, III, V, IV, II D. III, V, I, IV, II

13. I. Like Lord Byron a century earlier, he had learn to play himself, his own best hero, with superb conviction. 13.____
II. Or maybe he was Tarzan Hemingway, crouching in the African bush with elephant gun at the ready.
III. He was Hemingway of the rugged outdoor grin and the hairy chest posing beside the lion he had just shot.
IV. But even without the legend, the chest-beating, wisecracking pose that was later to seem so absurd, his impact upon us was tremendous.
V. By the time we were old enough to read Hemingway, he had become legendary.
The CORRECT answer is:
A. I, V, II, IV, III B. II, I, III, IV, V C. IV, II, V, III, I D. V, I, III, II, IV

14. I. Why do the electrons that inhabit atoms jump around so strangely, from one bizarrely shaped orbital to another? 14.____
II. And most importantly, why do protons, the bits that give atoms their heft and personality, stick together at all?
III. Why are some atoms, like sodium, so hyperactive while others, like helium, are so aloof?
IV. As any good contractor will tell you, a sound structure requires stable materials.
V. But atoms, the building blocks of everything we know and love—brownies and butterflies and beyond—do not appear to be models of stability.
The CORRECT answer is:
A. IV, V, III, I, II B. V, III, I, II, IV C. I, IV, II, V, III D. III, I, IV, II, V

15. I. Current atomic theory suggests that the strong nuclear force is most likely conveyed by massless particles called "gluons". 15.____
II. According to quantum chromodynamics (QCD), protons and neutrons are composed of smaller particles called quarks, which are held together by the gluons.
III. As a quantum theory, it conceives of space and time as tiny chunks that occasionally misbehave, rather than smooth predictable quantities.

IV. If you are hoping that QCD ties up atomic behavior with a tidy little bow, you will be disappointed.
V. This quark-binding force has "residue" that extends beyond protons and neutrons themselves to provide enough force to bind the protons and neutrons together.

The CORRECT answer is:
A. III, IV, II, V, I B. II, I, IV, III, V C. I, II, V, IV, III D. V, III, I, IV, II

16. I. I have seen him whip a woman, causing the blood to run half an hour at a time. 16.____
II. Mr. Severe, the overseer, used to stand by the door of the quarter, armed with a large hickory stick, ready to whip anyone who was not ready to start at the sound of the horn.
III. This was in the midst of her crying children, pleading for their mother's release.
IV. He seemed to take pleasure in manifesting his fiendish barbarity.
V. Mr. Severe was rightly named: he was a cruel man.

The CORRECT answer is:
A. I, IV, III, II, I B. II, V, I, III, IV C. II, V, III, I, IV D. IV, III, I, V, II

17. I. His death was recorded by the slaves as the result of a merciful providence. 17.____
II. His career was cut short.
III. He died very soon after I went to Colonel Lloyd's; and he died as he lived, uttering bitter curses and horrid oaths.
IV. Mr. Severe's place was filled by a Mr. Hopkins.
V. From the rising till the going down of the sun, he was cursing, raving, cutting, and slashing among the slaves in the field.

The CORRECT answer is:
A. V, II, III, I, IV B. IV, I, III, II, V C. III, I, IV, V, II D. I, II, V, III, IV

18. I. The primary reef-building organisms are invertebrate animals known as corals. 18.____
II. They are located in warm, shallow, tropical marine waters with enough light to stimulate the growth of reef organisms.
III. Coral reefs are highly diverse ecosystems, supporting greater numbers of fish species than any other marine ecosystem.
IV. They belong to the class Anthozoa and are subdivided into stony corals, which have six tentacles.
V. These corals are small colonial, marine invertebrates.

The CORRECT answer is:
A. I, IV, V, II, III B. V, I, III, IV, II C. III, II, I, V, IV D. IV, V, II, III, I

19. I. Jane Goodall, an English ethologist, is famous for her studies of the chimpanzees of the Gombe Stream Reserve in Tanzania. 19.____
II. As a result of her studies, Goodall concluded that chimpanzees are an advanced species closely related to humans.
III. Ultimately, Goodall's observations led her to write *The Chimpanzee Family Book*, which conveys a new, more humane view of wildlife.

IV. She is credited with the first recorded observation of chimps eating meat and using and making tools.
V. Her observations have forced scientists to redefine the characteristics once considered as solely human traits.

The CORRECT answer is:
A. V, II, IV, III, I B. I, IV, II, V, III C. I, II, V, IV, III D. III, V, II, I, IV

20. I. Since then, research has demonstrated that the deposition of atmospheric chemicals is causing widespread acidification of lakes, streams, and soil. 20.____
II. "Acid rain" is a popularly used phrase that refers to the deposition of acidifying substances from the atmosphere.
III. This phenomenon became a prominent issue around 1970.
IV. Of the many chemicals that are deposited from the atmosphere, the most important in terms of causing acidity in soil and surface waters are dilute solutions of sulfuric and nitric acids.
V. These chemicals are deposited as acidic rain or snow and include sulfur dioxide, oxides of nitrogen, and tiny particulates such as ammonium sulfate.

The CORRECT answer is:
A. III, IV, I, II, V B. IV, III, I, IV, V C. V, I, IV, III, II D. II, III, I, IV, V

21. I. Programmers wrote algorithmic software that precisely specified both the problem and how to solve it. 21.____
II. AI programmers, in contrast, have sought to program computers with flexible rules for seeking solutions to problems.
III. In the 1940 and 1950s, the first large, electronic, digital computers were designed to perform numerical calculations set up by a human programmer.
IV. The computers did so by completing a series of clearly defined steps, or algorithms.
V. An AI program may be designed to modify the rules it is given or to develop entirely new rules.

The CORRECT answer is:
A. I, III, II, V, IV B. IV, I, III, V, II C. III, IV, I, II, V D. III, I, II, IV, V

22. I. Wildfire is a periodic ecological disturbance, associated with the rapid combustion of much of the biomass of an ecosystem. 22.____
II. Wildfires themselves are both routine and ecologically necessary.
III. It is where they encounter human habitation, of course, that dangers quickly escalate,
IV. Once ignited by lightning or by humans, the biomass oxidizes as an uncontrolled blaze.
V. This unfettered burning continues until the fire either runs out of fuel or is quenched.

The CORRECT answer is:
A. V, IV, I, II, III B. I, II, V, III, IV C. III, II, I, IV, V D. IV, V, III, I, II

23. I. His arguments supported the positions advanced by the Democratic Party's southern wing and sharply challenged the constitutionality of the Republican Party's emerging political platform. 23.____
II. Beginning in the mid-1840s as a simple freedom suit, the case ended with the Court's intervention in the central political issues of the 1850s and the intensification of the sectional crisis that ultimately led to civil war.
III. During the Civil War, the decision quickly fell into disrepute, and its major rulings were overruled by ratification of the 13th and 14th Amendments.
IV. *Dred Scott v. Sandford* ranks as one of the worst decisions in the Supreme Court's history.
V. Chief Justice Roger Taney, speaking for a deeply divided Court, brought about this turn of events by ruling that no black American—whether free or enslaved—could be a U.S. citizen and that Congress possessed no legitimate authority to prohibit slavery's expansion into the federal territories.
The CORRECT answer is:
A. II, IV, I, III, V B. V, I, III, IV, II C. I, V, II, V, III D. IV, II, V, I, III

24. I. Considered the last battle between the U.S. Army and American Indians, the Wounded Knee Massacre took place on the morning of 29 December 1890 beside Wounded Knee Creek on South Dakota's Pine Ridge Reservation. 24.____
II. This was the culmination of the Ghost Dance religion that had started with a Paiute prophet from Nevada named Wovoka (1856-1932), who was also known as Jack Wilson.
III. During the previous year, U.S. government officials had reduced Sioux lands and cut back rations so severely that the Sioux people were starving.
IV. These conditions encouraged the desperate embrace of the Ghost Dance.
V. This pan-tribal ritual had historical antecedents that go much further back than its actual founder.
The CORRECT answer is:
A. I, II, III, IV, V B. V, IV, II, III, I C. IV, III, I, V, II D. III, I, V, II, IV

25. I. Their actions, which became known as the Boston Tea Party, set in motion events that led directly to the American Revolution. 25.____
II. Urged on by a crowd of cheering townspeople, the disguised Bostonians destroyed 342 chests of tea estimated to be worth between $10,000 an $18,000.
III. The Americans, who numbered around 70, shared a common aim: to destroy the ships' cargo of British East India Company tea.
IV. Many years later, George Hewes, a 31-year-old shoemaker and participant, recalled "We then were ordered by our commander to open the hatches and take out all the chests of tea and throw them overboard. And we immediately proceeded to execute his orders, first cutting and splitting the chests with our tomahawks, so as thoroughly to expose them to the effects of the water.

V. At nine o'clock on the night of December 16, 1773, a band of Bostonians disguised as Native Americans boarded the British merchant ship Dartmouth and two companion vessels anchored at Griffin's Wharf in Boston harbor.

The CORRECT answer is:

A. V, III, IV, II, I B. IV, II, III, I, V C. III, IV, V, II, I D. V, II, IV, III, I

KEY (CORRECT ANSWERS)

1.	A	11.	A
2.	C	12.	D
3.	D	13.	D
4.	B	14.	A
5.	C	15.	C
6.	D	16.	B
7.	B	17.	A
8.	A	18.	C
9.	C	19.	B
10.	B	20.	D

21.	C
22.	B
23.	D
24.	A
25.	A

TEST 2

DIRECTIONS: The sentences listed below are part of a meaningful paragraph, but they are not given in their proper order. You are to decide what would be the BEST order to put sentences to form a well-organized paragraph. Each sentence has a place in the paragraph; there are no extra sentences. *PRINT THE LETTER OF THE CORRECT ANSWER IN THE SPACE AT THE RIGHT.*

1. I. Recently, some U.S. cities have added a new category: compost, organic matter such as food scraps and yard debris. 1.____
   II. For example, paper may go in one container, glass and aluminum in another, regular garbage in a third.
   III. Like paper or glass recycling, compositing demands a certain amount of effort from the public in order to be successful.
   IV. Over the past generation, people in many parts of the United States have become accustomed to dividing their household waste products into different categories for recycling.
   V. But the inconveniences of composting are far outweighed by its benefits.
   The CORRECT answer is:
   A. V, II, III, IV, I B. I, III, IV, V, II C. IV, II, I, III, V D. III, I, V, II, IV

2. I. It also enhances soil texture, encouraging healthy roots and minimizing the need for chemical fertilizers. 2.____
   II. Most people think of banana peels, eggshells, and dead leaves as "waste," but compost is actually a valuable resource with multiple practical uses.
   III. When utilized as a garden fertilizer, compost provides nutrients to soil and improves plant growth while deterring or killing pests and preventing some plant diseases.
   IV. In large quantities, compost can be converted into a natural gas that can be used as fuel for transportation or heating and cooling systems.
   V. Better than soil at holding moisture, compost minimizes water waste and storm runoff, increases savings on watering costs, and helps reduce erosion on embankments near bodies of water.
   The CORRECT answer is:
   A. II, III, I, V, IV B. I, IV, V, III, II C. V, II, IV, I,III D. III, V, II, IV, I

3. I. The street is a sea of red, the traditional Chinese color of luck and happiness. 3.____
   II. Buildings are draped with festive, red banners and garlands.
   III. Crowds gather then to celebrate Lunar New Year.
   IV. Lamp posts are strung with crimson paper lanterns, which bob in the crisp winter breeze.
   V. At the beginning of February, thousands of people line H Street, the heart of Chinatown in Washington, D.C.
   The CORRECT answer is:
   A. I, V, II, III, IV B. IV, II, V, I, III C. III, I, II, IV, V D. V, III, I, II, IV

4. I. Experts agree that the lion dance originated in the Han dynasty; however, there is little agreement about the dance's original purpose. 4.____
   II. Another theory is that an emperor, upon waking from a dream about a lion, hired an artist to choreograph the dance.
   III. Dancers must be synchronized with the music accompanying the dance, as well as with each other, in order to fully realize the celebration.
   IV. Whatever the origins are, the current function of the dance is celebration.
   V. Some evidence suggests that the earliest version of the dance was an attempt to ward off an evil spirt.
   The CORRECT answer is:
   A. V, II, IV, III, I B. I, V, II, IV, III C. II, I, III, V, IV D. IV, III, V, I, II

5. I. Half the population of New York, Toronto, and London do not own cars; instead they use public transport. 5.____
   II. Every day, subway systems carry 155 million passengers, thirty-four times the number carried by all the world's airplanes.
   III. Though there are 600 million cars on the planet, and counting, there are also seven billion people, which means most of us get around taking other modes of transportation.
   IV. All of that is to say that even a century and a half after the invention of the internal combustion engine, private car ownership is still an anomaly.
   V. In other words, traveling to work, school, or the market means being a straphanger: someone who relies on public transport.
   The CORRECT answer is:
   A. I, II, IV, V, III B. III, V, I, II, IV C. III, I, II, IV, V D. II, IV, V, III, I

6. I. "They jumped up like popcorn," he said, describing how they would flap their half-formed wings and take short hops into the air. 6.____
   II. Dan settled on the Chukar Partridge as a model species, but he might not have made his discovery without the help of a local rancher that supplied him with the birds.
   III. At field sites around the world, Dan Kiel saw a pattern in how young ground birds ran along behind their parents.
   IV. So when a group of graduate students challenged him to come up with new data on the age-old ground-up-tree-down debate, he designed a project to see what clues might lie in how baby game birds learned to fly.
   V. When the rancher stopped by to see how things were progressing, he yelled at Dan to give the birds something to climb on.
   The CORRECT answer is:
   A. IV, II, V, I, III B. III, II, I, V, IV C. III, I, IV, II, V D. I, II, IV, V, III

7. I. Honey bees are hosts to the pathogenic large ectoparasitic mite, *Varroa destructor*. 7.____
   II. These mites feed on bee hemolymph (blood) and can kill bees directly or by increasing their susceptibility to secondary infections.
   III. Little is known about the natural defenses that keep the mite infections under control.

IV. Pyrethrums are a group of flowering plants that produce potent insecticides with anti-mite activity.
V. In fact, the human mite infestation known as scabies is treated with a topical pyrethrum cream.

The CORRECT answer is:
A. I, II, III, IV, V B. V, IV, II, I, III C. III, IV, V, I, II D. II, IV, I, III, V

8. I. He hardly ever allowed me to pay for the books he placed in my hands, but when he wasn't looking I'd leave the coins I'd managed to collect on the counter. 8.____
II. My favorite place in the whole city was the Sempere & Sons bookshop on Calle Santa Ana.
III. It smelled of old paper and dust and it was my sanctuary, my refuge.
IV. The bookseller would let me sit on a chair in a corner and read any book I liked to my heart's content.
V. It was only small change—if I'd had to buy a book with that pittance, I would probably have been able to afford only a booklet of cigarette papers.

The CORRECT answer is:
A. I, III, V, II, IV B. II, IV, I, III, V C. V, I, III, IV, II D. II, III, IV, I, V

9. I. At school, I had learned to read and write long before the other children. 9.____
II. My father, however, did not see things the way I did; he did not like to see books in the house.
III. Where my school friends saw notches of ink on incomprehensible pages, I saw light, streets, and people.
IV. Back then my only friends were made of paper and ink.
V. Words and the mystery of their hidden science fascinated me, and I saw in them a key with which I could unlock a boundless world.

The CORRECT answer is:
A. IV, I, III, V, II B. I, V, III, IV, II C. II, I, V, III, IV D. V, IV, II, III, I

10. I. Gary King of Harvard University says that one main reason null results are not published is because there were many ways to produce them by messing up. 10.____
II. Oddly enough, there is little hard data on how often or why null results are squelched.
III. The various errors make the null reports almost impossible to predict, Mr. King believes.
IV. In recent years, the debate has spread to social and behavioral science, which help sway public and social policy.
V. The question of what to do with null results in research has long been hotly debated among those conducting medical trials.

The CORRECT answer is:
A. I, III, IV, V, II B. V, I, II, IV, III C. III, II, I, V, IV D. V, IV, II, I, III

11. I. In a recent study, Stanford political economist Neil Malholtra and two of his graduate students examined all studies funded by TESS (Time-sharing Experiments for Social Sciences). 11.____

II. Scientists of these experiments cited deeper problems within their studies but also believed many journalists wouldn't be interested in their findings.

III. TESS allows scientists to order up internet-based surveys of a representative sample of U.S. adults to test a particular hypothesis.

IV. One scientist went on record as saying, "The reality is that null effects do not tell a clear story."

V. Well, Malholtra's team tracked down working papers from most of the experiments that weren't published to find out what had happened to their results.

The CORRECT answer is:

A. IV, II, V, III, I B. I, III, V, II, IV C. III, V, I, IV, II D. I, III, IV, II, V

12. I. The work also suggests that these ultra-tiny salt wires may already exist in sea spray and large underground salt deposits. 12.____

II. Scientists expect for metals such as gold or lead to stretch out at temperatures well below their melting points, but they never expected this superplasticity in a rigid, crystalline material like salt.

III. Inflexible old salt becomes a softy in the nanoworld, stretching like taffy to more than twice its length, researchers report.

IV. The findings may lead to new approaches for making nanowires that could end up in solar cells or electronic circuits.

V. According to Nathan Moore of Sandia National Laboratories, these nanowires are special and much more common than we may think.

The CORRECT answer is:

A. IV, III, V, II, I B. I, V, III, IV, II C. III, IV, I, V, II D. V, II, III, I, IV

13. I. The Venus flytrap (Dionaea muscipula) needs to know when an ideal meal is crawling across its leaves. 13.____

II. The large black hairs on their lobes allow the Venus flytraps to literally feel their prey, and they act as triggers that spring the trap closed.

III. To be clear, if an insect touches just one hair, the trap will not spring shut; but a large enough bug will likely touch two hairs within twenty seconds which is the signal the Venus flytrap waits for.

IV. Closing its trap requires a huge expense of energy, and reopening can take several hours.

V. When the proper prey makes its way across the trap, the Dionaea launches into action.

The CORRECT answer is:

A. IV, I, V, II, III B. II, V, I, III, IV C. I, II, V, IV, III D. I, IV, II, V, III

14. I. These books usually contain collections of stories, many of which are much older than the books themselves. 14.____
    II. Where other early European authors wrote their literary works in Latin, the Irish began writing down their stories in their own language as early as 6th century B.C.E.
    III. Ireland has the oldest vernacular literature in Europe.
    IV. One of the most famous of these collections is the epic cycle, *The Táin Bó Culainge*, which translates to "The Cattle Raid of Cooley."
    V. While much of the earliest Irish writing has been lost or destroyed, several manuscripts survive from the late medieval period.

    The CORRECT answer is:
    A. V, IV, I, II, III B. III, II, V, I, IV C. III, I, IV, V, II D. IV, II, III, I, V

15. I. Obviously the plot is thin, but it works better as a thematic peace, exploring several great issues that plagued authors and people during that era. 15.____
    II. The story begins during a raid when Meb's forces are joined by Frederick and his men.
    III. In the end, many warriors on both sides perish, the prize is lost, and peace is somehow re-established between the opposing sides.
    IV. The middle of the story tells of how Chulu fends off Meb's army by herself while Concho's men struggle against witchcraft.
    V. The prize is defended by the current king, Concho, and the young warrior, Chulu.

    The CORRECT answer is:
    A. II, V, IV, III, I B. V, I, IV, III, II C. I, III, V, IV, II D. III, II, I, V, IV

16. I. However, sometimes the flowers that are treated with the pesticides are not as vibrant as those that did not receive the treatment. 16.____
    II. The first phase featured no pesticides and the second featured a pesticide that varied in doses.
    III. In the cultivation of roses, certain pesticides are often applied when the presence of aphids is detected.
    IV. Recently, researchers conducted two phases of an experiment to study the effects of certain pesticides on rose bushes.
    V. To start, aphids are small plant-eating insects known to feed on rose bushes.

    The CORRECT answer is:
    A. IV, III, II, I, V B. I, II, V, III, IV C. V, III, I, IV, II D. II, V, IV, I, III

17. I. My passion for it took hold many years ago when I happened to cross paths with a hiker in a national park. 17.____
    II. The wilderness has a way of cleansing the spirit.
    III. His excitement was infectious as he quoted various poetic verses pertaining to the wild; I was hooked.
    IV. For some, backpacking is the ultimate vacation.
    V. While it once felt tedious and tiring, backpacking is now an essential part of my summer recreation.

    The CORRECT answer is:
    A. IV, II, V, I, III B. II, III, I, IV, V C. I, IV, II, V, III D. V, I, III, II, IV

18. I. When I was preparing for my two-week vacation to southern Africa, I realized that the continent would be like nothing I have ever seen. 18.____
II. I wanted to explore the continent's urban streets as well as the savannah; it's always been my dream to have "off the grid" experiences as well as touristy ones.
III. The largest gap in understanding came from an unlikely source; it was the way I played with my host family's dog.
IV. Upon my arrival to Africa, the people I met welcomed me with open arms.
V. Aside from the pleasant welcome, it was obvious that our cultural differences were stark, which led to plenty of laughter and confusion.
The CORRECT answer is:
A. IV, I, II, III, V B. III, V, IV, II, I C. I, IV, II, III, V D. I, II, IV, V, III

19. I. There, I signed up for a full-contact, downhill ice-skating race that looked like a bobsled run. 19.____
II. It wasn't until I took a trip to Montreal that I realized how wrong I was.
III. As an avid skier and inline skater, I figured I had cornered the market on downhill speeds.
IV. After avoiding hip and body checks, both of which were perfectly legal, I was able to reach a top speed of forty-five miles per hour!
V. It was Carnaval season, the time when people from across the province flock to the city for two weeks of food, drink and winter sports.
The CORRECT answer is:
A. II, I, III, IV, V B. III, II, V, I, IV C. IV, V, I, III, II D. I, IV, II, V, III

20. I. It is a spell that sets upon one's soul and a sense of euphoria is felt by all who experience it. 20.____
II. Pictures and postcards of the Caribbean do not lie; the water there shines with every shade of aquamarine, from pastel to emerald.
III. As I imagine these sights, I recall one trip in particular that neatly captures the allure of the Caribbean.
IV. The ocean hypnotizes with its glassy vastness.
V. On that beautiful day, I was incredibly happy to sail with my family and friends.
The CORRECT answer is:
A. I, V, IV, III, II B. V, I, II, IV, III C. II, IV, I, III, V D. I, II, IV, III, V

21. I. It wasn't until the early 1700s that it began to resemble the masterpiece museum it is today. 21.____
II. The Louvre contains some of the most famous works of art in the history of the world including the *Mona Lisa* and the *Venus de Milo*.
III. Before it was a world famous museum, The Louvre was a fort built by King Philip sometime around 1200 A.D.
IV. The Louvre, in Paris, France, is one of the largest museums in the world.
V. It has almost 275,000 works of art, which are displayed in over 140 exhibition rooms.
The CORRECT answer is:
A. V, I, III, IV, II B. II, IV, I, V, III C. V, III, I, IV, II D. IV, V, II, III, I

22. I. It danced on the glossy hair and bright eyes of two girls, who sat together hemming ruffles for a white muslin dress. 22.____
II. The September sun was glinting cheerfully into a pretty bedroom furnished with blue.
III. These girls were Clover and Elsie Carr, and it was Clover's first evening dress for which they were hemming ruffles.
IV. The half-finished skirt of the dress lay on the bed, and as each crisp ruffle was completed, the girls added it to the snowy heap, which looked like a drift of transparent clouds.
V. It was nearly two years since a certain visit made by Johnnie to Inches Mills and more than three since Clover and Katy had returned home from the boarding school at Hillsover.
The CORRECT answer is:
A. III, V, IV, I, II B. II, I, IV, III, V C. V, II, I, IV, III D. II, IV, III, I, V

23. I. The "invisible hand" theory is harshly criticized by parties who argue that untampered self-interest is immoral and that charity is the superior vehicle for community improvement. 23.____
II. Standing as a testament to his benevolence, Smith bequeathed much of his wealth to charity.
III. Second, Smith was not arguing that all self-interest is positive for society; he simply did not agree that it was necessarily bad.
IV. First, he was not declaring that people should adopt a pattern of overt self-interest, but rather that people already act in such a way.
V. Some of these people, though, fail to recognize several important aspects of Adam Smith's the Scottish economist who championed this theory, concept.
The CORRECT answer is:
A. I, V, IV, III, II B. III, IV, II, I, V C. II, III, V, IV, I D. IV, III, I, V, II

24. I. Though they rarely are awarded for their many accomplishments, composers and performers continue to innovate and represent a substantial reason for classical music's persistent popularity. 24.____
II. It is often the subject of experimentation on the part of composers and performers.
III. Even more restrictive is the mainstream definition of "classical," which only includes the music of generations past that has seemingly been pushed aside by such contemporary forms of music as jazz, rock, and rap.
IV. In spite of its waning limelight, however, classical music occupies an enduring niche in Western culture.
V. Many people take classical music to be the realm of the symphony orchestra or smaller ensembles of orchestral instruments.
The CORRECT answer is:
A. IV, I, III, II, V B. II, IV, V, I, III C. V, III, IV, II, I D. I, V, III, IV, II

25. I. The Great Pyramid at Giza is arguably one of the most fascinating and contentious pieces of architecture in the world. 25.____
II. Instead of clarifying or expunging older theories about its age, the results of the study left the researchers mystified.
III. In the 1980s, researchers began focusing on studying the mortar from the pyramid, hoping it would reveal important clues about the pyramid's age and construction.
IV. This discovery was controversial because these dates claimed that the structure was built over 400 years earlier than most archaeologists originally believed it had been constructed.
V. Carbon dating revealed that the pyramid had been built between 3100 BCE and 2850 BCE with an average date of 2977 BCE.

The CORRECT answer is:
A. I, III, II, V, IV B. II, III, IV, V, I C. V, I, III, IV, II D. III, IV, V, I, II

KEY (CORRECT ANSWERS)

1.	C	11.	B
2.	A	12.	C
3.	D	13.	D
4.	B	14.	B
5.	B	15.	A
6.	C	16.	C
7.	A	17.	A
8.	D	18.	D
9.	A	19.	B
10.	D	20.	C

21.	D
22.	B
23.	A
24.	C
25.	A

EXAMINATION SECTION

TEST 1

DIRECTIONS: The sentences listed below are part of a meaningful paragraph, but they are not given in their proper order. You are to decide what would be the BEST order to put sentences to form a well-organized paragraph. Each sentence has a place in the paragraph; there are no extra sentences. *PRINT THE LETTER OF THE CORRECT ANSWER IN THE SPACE AT THE RIGHT.*

Questions 1-3.

DIRECTIONS: Questions 1 through 3 are to be answered on the basis of the following passage.

Almost half of the increase in Chicago came from five neighborhoods, including West Garfield Park. He was 12 years old and had just been recruited into a gang by his older brothers and cousin. A decade later, he sits in Cook County jail, held without bail and awaiting trial on three cases, including felony drug charges and possession of a weapon. Violence in Chicago erupted last year, with the city recording 771 murders—a 58% jump from 2015. They point to a $95 million police-training center in West Garfield Park, public-transit improvements on Chicago's south side and efforts to get major corporations such as Whole Foods and Wal-Mart to invest. Chicago city officials say that they are making strategic investments in ailing neighborhoods. Amarley Coggins remembers the first time he dealt heroin, discreetly approaching a car coming off an interstate highway and into West Garfield park, the neighborhood where he grew up on Chicago's west side.

1. When organized correctly, the first sentence of the paragraph begins with 1.____
   A. "Amarley Coggins remembers..." B. "He was 12 years old..."
   C. "They point to a..." D. "Violence in Chicago..."

2. After correctly organizing the paragraph, the author wishes to replace a word in the last sentence with its synonym *enterprises*. Which word does the author wish to replace? 2.____
   A. murders B. neighborhoods
   C. corporations D. improvements

3. If put together correctly, the second to last sentence would end with the words 3.____
   A. "...Chicago's west side." B. "...in ailing neighborhoods."
   C. "...older brother and cousins." D. "...and Wal-Mart to invest."

Questions 4-6.

DIRECTIONS: Questions 4 through 6 are to be answered on the basis of the following passage.

Critics argue that driverless vehicles pose too many risks, including cyberattacks, computer malfunctions, relying on algorithms to make ethical decisions, and fewer transportation jobs. Driverless vehicles, also called autonomous vehicles and self-driving vehicles, are vehicles that can operate without human intervention. And algorithms make decisions based on data obtained from sensors and connectivity. Driverless vehicles rely primarily on three technologies: sensors, connectivity, and algorithms. Sensors observe multiple directions simultaneously. Connectivity accesses information on traffic, weather, road hazards, and navigation. Supporters argue that driverless vehicles have many benefits, including fewer traffic accidents and fatalities, more efficient traffic flows, greater mobility for those who cannot drive, and less pollution. Once the realm of science fiction, driverless vehicles could revolutionize automotive travel over the next few decades.

4. When all of the sentences are organized in correct order, the first sentence starts with 4.____
   A. "Connectivity accesses information..."
   B. "Critics argue that..."
   C. "Once the realm of..."
   D. "Driverless vehicles, also called..."

5. If the above paragraph appeared in correct order, which of the following transition words would be MOST appropriate in the beginning of the sentence that starts "Critics argue that..." 5.____
   A. Additionally
   B. To begin,
   C. In conclusion,
   D. Conversely,

6. When the paragraph is properly arranged, it ends with the words 6.____
   A. "...over the next few decades."
   B. "...fewer transportation jobs."
   C. "...and less pollution."
   D. "...without human intervention"

Questions 7-10.

DIRECTIONS: Questions 7 through 10 are to be answered on the basis of the following passage.

This method had some success, but also carried fatal risks. Various people across Europe independently developed vaccination as an alternative during the later years of the eighteenth century, but Edward Jenner (1749-1823) popularized the practice. Vaccination has been called a miracle of modern medicine, but it has a long and controversial history stretching back to the ancient world. In 1803 the Royal Jennerian Institute was founded in England, and vaccination programs initially drew enormous public support. In 429 BCE in Greece, the historian Thucydides (c.460-c.395 BCE) noted that survivors of smallpox did not become reinfected in subsequent epidemics. Variolation as a means of preventing severe smallpox infection became an accepted practice in China in the tenth century CE, and its popularity spread across Asia,

Europe, and to the Americas by the seventeenth century. Variolation required either inhalation of smallpox dust, or putting scabs or parts of the smallpox pustules under the skin. Widespread inoculation against smallpox was purported to have been part of Ayurvedic tradition as far back as at least 1000 BCE, when Indian doctors traveled to households before the rainy season each year.

7. When arranged properly, what does "This method" refer to in the sentence that begins "This method had some success..."? 7.____
   A. Vaccination B. Inoculation
   C. Variolation D. Hybridization

8. When organized correctly, the paragraph's third sentence should begin 8.____
   A. "In 429 BCE in Greece..." B. "Variolation required..."
   C. "In 1803 the..." D. "Vaccination has been called..."

9. If put in the correct order, this paragraph should end with the words 9.____
   A. "...under the skin." B. "...to the ancient world."
   C. "...enormous public support." D. "...by the seventeenth century."

10. In the second sentence, the author is thinking about using the word immunization instead of which of its synonyms? 10.____
    A. Variolation B. Vaccination C. Inhalation D. Inoculation

Questions 11-13.

DIRECTIONS: Questions 11 through 13 are to be answered on the basis of the following passage.

Summers are hot—often north of 100 degrees—and because it lies at the far end of a San Diego Gas & Electric transmission line, the town has suffered frequent power outages. Another way is that microgrids can ease the entry of intermittent renewable energy sources, like wind and solar, into the modern grid. Utilities are also interested in microgrids because of the money they can save by deferring the need to build new transmission lines. "If you're on the very end of a utility line, everything that happens, happens 10 times worse for you," says Mike Gravely, team leader for energy systems integration at the California Energy Commission. The town has a lot of senior citizens, who can be frail in the heat. Borrego Springs, California, is a quaint town of about 3,400 people set against the Anza-Borrego Desert about 90 miles east of San Diego. High winds, lightning strikes, forest fires and flash floods can bust up that line and kill the electricity. But today, Borrego Springs has a failsafe against power outages: a microgrid. Resiliency is one of the main reasons the market in microgrids is booming, with installed capacity in the United States projected to be more than double between 2017 and 2022, according to a new report on microgrids from GTM Research. "Without air conditioning," says Linda Haddock, head of the local Chamber of Commerce, "people will die."

11. When the sentences above are organized correctly, the paragraph should start with the sentence that begins 11.____
    A. "Borrego Springs, California..." B. "But today, Borrego Springs..."
    C. "Summers are hot..." D. "Utilities are also interested..."

12. If the author wanted to split this paragraph into two smaller paragraphs, the first sentence of the second paragraph would start with the words 12.____
    A. "High winds, lightning strikes, forest fires..."
    B. "But today, Borrego Springs..."
    C. "Resiliency is one of the main..."
    D. "If you're on the very end..."

13. Assuming the paragraph were organized correctly, the second to last sentence would end 13.____
    A. "...to build new transmission lines."
    B. "...be frail in the heat."
    C. "...into the modern grid."
    D. "...east of San Diego."

Questions 14-17.

DIRECTIONS: Questions 14 through 17 are to be answered on the basis of the following passage.

Exhaustive search is not typically a successful approach to problem solving because most interesting problems have search spaces that are simply too large to be dealt with in this manner, even by the fastest computers. Thus, in order to ignore a portion of a search space, some guiding knowledge or insight must exist so that the solution will not be overlooked. This partial understanding is reflected in the fact that a rigid algorithmic solution—a routine and predetermined number of computational steps—cannot be applied. A large part of the intelligence of chess players resides in the heuristics they employ. When search is used to explore the entire solution space, it is said to be exhaustive. Chess is a classic example where humans routinely employ sophisticated heuristics in a search space. Therefore, if one hopes to find a solution (or a reasonably good approximation of a solution) to such a problem, one must selectively explore the problem's search space. Rather, the concept of search is used to solve such problems. Heuristics is a major area of AI that concerns itself with how to limit effectively the exploration of a search space. Many problems that humans are confronted with are not fully understood. The difficulty here is that if part of the search space is not explored, one runs the risk that the solution one seeks will be missed. A chess player will typically search through a small number of possible moves before selecting a move to play. Not every possible move and countermove sequence is explored. Only reasonable sequences are examined.

14. When correctly organized, the paragraph above should begin with the words 14.____
    A. "Many problems that..."
    B. "Therefore, if one hopes to..."
    C. "Only reasonable sequences are..."
    D. "The difficulty here is..."

15. If the paragraph was organized correctly, the fourth sentence would begin with the words 15.____
    A. "Chess is a classic..."
    B. "Heuristics is a major..."
    C. "Exhaustive search is not..."
    D. "The difficulty here is..."

16. If the author wished to separate this paragraph into two equally sized paragraphs, the sentence that begins the second paragraph would END with the words 16.____
   A. "...heuristics they employ."
   B. "...in a search space."
   C. "...are not fully employed."
   D. "...will be missed."

17. When organized correctly, the paragraph would end with the words 17.____
   A. "...the heuristics they employ."
   B. "...will not be overlooked."
   C. "...said to be exhaustive."
   D. "...are not fully understood."

Questions 18-21.

DIRECTIONS: Questions 18 through 21 are to be answered on the basis of the following passage.

Asian-Americans soon found themselves the targets of ridicule and attacks. Prior to the bombing he had tried to enlist in the military but was turned down due to poor health. His case, Korematsu v. The United States, is still considered a blemish on the record of the Supreme Court and has received heightened scrutiny given the indefinite confinement of many prisoners after the terrorist attacks on September 11, 2001. On February 19, 1942, President Franklin D. Roosevelt issued Executive Order 9066, which granted the leaders of the armed forces permission to create Military Areas and authorizing the removal of any and all persons from those areas. Fred Korematsu was a 22-year-old welder when the Japanese bombed Pearl Harbor on December 7, 1941. A Nisei—which means an American citizen born to Japanese parents—he was one of four brothers and grew up working in his parents' plant nursery in Oakland, California. This statement effectively pronounced Japanese-Americans on the West Coast as traitors because even though Executive Order 9066 allowed the military to remove any person from designated areas, only those of Japanese descent were ordered to leave. Before Pearl Harbor, he was employed by a defense contractor in California. At the time of the attack, he was having a picnic with his Italian-American girlfriend. Asian-American Fred Korematsu (1919-2005) is most remembered for challenging the legality of Japanese internment during World War II. It was for this simple reason that he eventually became known as a civil rights leader. American reaction to an attack on United States' soil was both swift and harsh. Awarded the Presidential Medal of Honor, he is considered a leader of the civil rights movement in the United States. Roosevelt justified these actions in the opening paragraph of the order by declaring, "the successful prosecution of the war requires every possible protection against espionage, and against sabotage to national-defense material, national-defenses premises and national-defense utilities." Years later he told the San Francisco Chronicle, "I was just living my life, and that's what I wanted to do."

18. When put together correctly, the above paragraph would begin with the words 18.____
   A. "It was for this simple reason..."
   B. "A Nisei—which means..."
   C. "Awarded the Presidential Medal of Honor..."
   D. "Asian-American Fred Korematsu..."

19. If the author wished to separate this piece into two separate paragraphs, the sentence that would be the BEST way to start the second paragraph would begin with the words 19.____
    A. "Awarded the Presidential Medal of Honor..."
    B. "Fred Korematsu was a..."
    C. "Roosevelt justified these actions..."
    D. "Before Pearl Harbor, he was..."

20. In the sentence that begins "A Nisei—which means...", who does "he" refer to in the paragraph? 20.____
    A. Roosevelt
    B. A sibling of Korematsu
    C. Fred Korematsu
    D. Japanese-Americans on the West Coast

21. If organized correctly, the fourth sentence should begin with the words 21.____
    A. "At the time of the attack..."
    B. "His case, Korematsu v. The United States..."
    C. "Fred Korematsu was a..."
    D. "This statement effectively pronounced..."

22. When put together correctly, the last sentence of the paragraph should end with the words 22.____
    A. "...that's what I wanted to do."
    B. "...were ordered to leave."
    C. "...during World War II."
    D. "...was both swift and harsh."

Questions 23-25.

DIRECTIONS: Questions 23 through 25 are to be answered on the basis of the following passage.

Over the past two decades, her personal finances have been eroded by illness, divorce, the cost of raising two children, the housing bust, and the economic downturn. "There are more people attending college, more people taking out loans, and more people taking out a higher dollar amount of loans," says Matthew Ward, associate director of media relations at the New York Fed. Anderson, who is 57, told her complicated story at a recent Senate Aging Committee hearing (she's previously appeared on the CBS Evening News). Some 3 percent of U.S. households that are headed by a senior citizen now hold federal student debt, mostly debt they took on to finance their own educations, according to a new report from the Government Accountability Office (GAO), an independent agency. She hasn't been able to afford payments on her loans for nearly eight years. Rosemary Anderson has a master's degree, a good job at the University of California (Santa Cruz), and student loans that she could be paying off until she's 81. Student debt has risen across every age group over the past decade, according to a Federal Reserve Bank of New York analysis of credit report data... "As the baby boomers continue to move into retirement, the number of older Americans with defaulted loans will only continue to increase," the report warned. She first enrolled in college in her thirties.

23. When organized correctly, the first sentence should begin with the words 23.____
    A. "She first enrolled..."
    B. "Anderson, who is 57..."
    C. "Some 3 percent of..."
    D. "Rosemary Anderson has..."

24. If the author wished to split the paragraph into two paragraphs (not necessarily equal in length), the first sentence of the second paragraph would begin with the words 24.____
    A. "Some 3 percent of..."
    B. "There are more people..."
    C. "Over the past two decades..."
    D. "She first enrolled..."

25. When put in the correct order, the second to last sentence should end with the words 25.____
    A. "...an independent agency."
    B. "...of credit report data."
    C. "...at the New York Fed."
    D. "...in her thirties."

KEY (CORRECT ANSWERS)

1.	A	11.	A
2.	C	12.	B
3.	B	13.	C
4.	D	14.	A
5.	D	15.	C
6.	B	16.	D
7.	C	17.	A
8.	A	18.	D
9.	C	19.	B
10.	D	20.	C

21.	C
22.	B
23.	D
24.	A
25.	B

TEST 2

DIRECTIONS: The sentences listed below are part of a meaningful paragraph, but they are not given in their proper order. You are to decide what would be the BEST order to put sentences to form a well-organized paragraph. Each sentence has a place in the paragraph; there are no extra sentences. *PRINT THE LETTER OF THE CORRECT ANSWER IN THE SPACE AT THE RIGHT.*

Questions 1-3.

DIRECTIONS: Questions 1 through 3 are to be answered on the basis of the following passage.

According to the World Health Organization (WHO), exposure to ambient (outdoor) air pollution causes 3 million premature deaths around the world each year, largely due to heart and lung diseases. Air pollution also contributes to such environmental threats as smog, acid rain, depletion of the ozone layer, and global climate change. The U.S. Environmental Protection Agency (EPA) sets National Ambient Air Quality Standards (NAAQS) for those four pollutants as well as carbon monoxide (CO) and lead. The EPA also regulates 187 toxic air pollutants, such as asbestos, benzene, dioxin, and mercury. Finally, the EPA places limits on emissions of greenhouse gases like carbon dioxide (CO_2) and methane, which contribute to global climate change. The WHO has established Air Quality Guidelines (ACGs) to identify safe levels of exposure to the emission of four harmful air pollutants worldwide: particulate matter (PM), ozone (O_3), nitrogen dioxide (NO_2), and sulfur dioxide (SO_2). Since EPA criteria define the allowable concentrations of these six substances in ambient air throughout the United States, they are known as criteria air pollutants. Air pollution refers to the release into the air of chemicals and other substances, known as pollutants, that are potentially harmful to human health and the environment.

1. When organized correctly, the first sentence of this paragraph should begin 1.____
   A. "Air pollution refers…"
   B. "The EPA also regulates..,"
   C. "The WHO has established…"
   D. "According to the…"

2. When put in the correct order, the fourth sentence should end with the words 2.____
   A. "…to global climate change."
   B. "…as criteria air pollutants."
   C. "…nitrogen dioxide (NO_2), and sulfur dioxide (SO_2)."
   D. "…health and the environment."

3. If put in the most logical order, the paragraph would end with the words 3.____
   A. "…as criteria air pollutants."
   B. "…to global climate change."
   C. "…benzene, dioxin, and mercury."
   D. "…human health and the environment."

Questions 4-6.

DIRECTIONS: Questions 4 through 6 are to be answered on the basis of the following passage.

Although gentrification has been associated with some positive impacts, such as urban revitalization and lower crime rates, critics charge that it marginalizes racial and ethnic minorities and destroys the character of urban neighborhoods. British sociologist Ruth Glass is credited with coining the term "gentrification" in her 1964 book *London: Aspects of Change*, which described the transformation that occurred when members of the gentry (an elite or privileged social class) took over working-class districts of London. Gentrification is a type of neighborhood change, a broader term that encompasses various physical, demographic, social, and economic processes that affect distinct residential areas. The arrival of wealthier people leads to new economic development and an increase in property values and rent, which often makes housing unaffordable for longtime residents. Gentrification is a transformation process that typically occurs in urban neighborhoods when higher-income people move in and displace lower-income existing residents.

4. When organized in the correct order, the first sentence of the paragraph should begin with the words 4.____
   A. "Gentrification is a type of..."
   B. "British sociologist Ruth..."
   C. "The arrival of..."
   D. "Gentrification is a transformation..."

5. If put together in the correct order, the second to last sentence in the paragraph would end with the words 5.____
   A. "...lower-income existing residents."
   B. "...that affect distinct residential areas."
   C. "...character of urban neighborhoods."
   D. "...working-class districts of London."

6. If the author wished to change the beginning of the final sentence to "in the end." to better signal the finish of the paragraph, which of the following words would the phrase appear in front of? 6.____
   A. British
   B. Gentrification
   C. Although
   D. The

Questions 7-11.

DIRECTIONS: Questions 7 through 11 are to be answered on the basis of the following passage.

The primary signs of ADHD include a persistent pattern of inattention or hyperactivity lasting in duration for six months or longer with an onset before 12 years of age. Children with ADHD often experience peer rejection, neglect, or teasing and family interactions may contain high levels of discord and negative interactions (APA, 2013). Two primary types of the disorder include inattentive and hyperactive/impulsive, with a combined type when both inattention and hyperactivity occur together. Inattentive ADHD is evidenced by executive functioning deficits such as being off task, lacking sustained focus, and being disorganized. Hyperactive ADHD is evidenced by excessive talkativeness and fidgeting, with an inability to control impulses that may result in harm. Attention Deficit Hyperactivity Disorder (ADHD) is a commonly diagnosed childhood behavioral disorder affecting millions of children in the U.S. every year (National Institute of Mental Health [NIMH], 2012), with prevalence rates between 5% and 11% of the population. Other research has examined singular traits such as executive function deficits in the school setting, task performance in the school setting (Berk, 1986), driving and awareness of time. However, researching academic aspects of the school experience does not provide a comprehensive understanding of the systemic effects of ADHD in the school environment. Historically, much research on ADHD has focused on the academic impact of behavioral symptoms such as reading and mathematics. These behaviors are inappropriate for the child's age level and symptoms typically interfere with functioning in multiple environments.

7. If the author put the paragraph into a logical order, the first sentence would begin with the words 7.____
   A. "Inattentive ADHD is..."
   B. "Historically, much research..."
   C. "These behaviors are..."
   D. "Attention Deficit Hyperactivity Disorder..."

8. When put in the correct order, what does the author mean by "These behaviors" in the sentence that begins "These behaviors are..."? 8.____
   A. Inattention or hyperactivity
   B. Reading and Mathematics
   C. Peer rejection
   D. Sustained focus

9. If the author wished to split this paragraph into two paragraphs (not necessarily equal parts), the first sentence of the second paragraph would BEGIN with the words 9.____
   A. "Historically, much research..."
   B. "Other research has examined..."
   C. "Two primary types of..."
   D. "Inattentive ADHD is evidenced..."

10. When put in the correct order, the third sentence in the paragraph would END with the words 10.____
   A. "...an onset before 12 years of age."
   B. "...5% and 11% of the population."
   C. "...such as reading and mathematics."
   D. "...in multiple environments."

11. If the above paragraph was organized correctly, its ending words of the last sentence would be 11.____
   A. "...sustained focus, and being disorganized."
   B. "...an onset before 12 years of age."
   C. "...in the school environment."
   D. "...inattention and hyperactivity occur together."

Questions 12-15.

DIRECTIONS: Questions 12 through 15 are to be answered on the basis of the following passage.

Health care fraud imposes huge costs on society. In prosecutions of fraud, the DOJ employs the resources of its own criminal and civil divisions, as well as those of the U.S. Attorneys' Offices, HHS, and the FBI. The FBI estimates that health care fraud accounts for at least three and possibly up to ten percent of total health care expenditures, or somewhere between $82 billion and $272 billion each year. Providers are also careful to screen hires for excluded persons or entities lest they be subject to civil monetary penalties. Several government agencies are involved in fighting health care fraud. Individual states assist the HHS Office of the Inspector General ("OIG") and Centers for Medicare & Medicaid Services ("CMS") to initiate and pursue investigations of Medicare and Medicaid fraud. In addition, the OIG uses its permissive exclusion authority to exclude individuals and entities convicted of health care related crimes from federally funded health care services in order to induce providers to help track fraud through a voluntary disclosure program. $30 to $98 billion dollars of that (approximately 36%) is fraud against the public health programs Medicare and Medicaid. The Department of Justice ("DOJ") and the Department of Health and Human Services ("HHS") enforce federal health care fraud law and regulations.

12. When put together in a logical order, the second sentence of the paragraph would end with the words 12.____
    A. "...in fighting health care fraud."
    B. "...$272 billion each year."
    C. "...voluntary disclosure program."
    D. "...to civil monetary penalties."

13. In order to organize the paragraph correctly, the sentence that begins "In addition, the OIG..." should FOLLOW the sentence that begins with the words 13.____
    A. "$30 to $98 billion dollars of that..."
    B. "Health care fraud..."
    C. "Individual states assist..."
    D. "In prosecutions of fraud..."

14. The author wishes to split the paragraph into a smaller introductory paragraph followed by a slightly longer body paragraph. Which of the following sentences would be BEST to start the second paragraph? 14.____
    A. "$30 to $98 billion dollars of that (approximately 36%) is fraud against the public health care programs Medicare and Medicaid."
    B. "Several government agencies are involved in fighting health care fraud."
    C. "In prosecutions of fraud, the DOJ employs the resources of its own criminal and civil divisions, as well as those of the U.S. Attorneys' Offices, HHS, and the FBI."
    D. "Health care fraud imposes huge costs on society."

15. If put together correctly, the paragraph should end with the words 15.____
   A. "...Attorneys' Offices, HHS, and the FBI."
   B. "...huge costs on society."
   C. "...fighting health care fraud."
   D. "...of Medicare and Medicaid fraud."

Questions 16-19.

DIRECTIONS: Questions 16 through 19 are to be answered on the basis of the following passage.

President Abraham Lincoln advocated for granting amnesty to former Confederates to heal the country after the devastating war. Adams and his fellow Federalist Party members in Congress used the law to jail more than a dozen of his political rivals. In 1977, President Jimmy Carter lifted the restrictions on draft dodgers, granting them unconditional amnesty. The issue of amnesty again arose shortly after the U.S. Civil War (1861-1865). Some U.S. government officials, including Vice President Andrew Johnson, advocating placing severe punishments on the military and civilian leaders of the secessionist Confederate States of America. A century later, the controversial nature of the Vietnam War (1964-1975), combined with the compulsory draft for military service, compelled many young men of eligible age to violate the law to avoid the draft. When Thomas Jefferson, Adams' Vice President and opponent of the Alien and Sedition Acts, won the 1800 presidential election, he declared amnesty for those found to have violated the law. Other young men who were drafted deserted the army and refused to serve. In May 1865, when serving as president following Lincoln's assassination, Johnson issued the Proclamation of Amnesty and Reconstruction, which granted the rights of voting and holding office to most former Confederates. In 1974, President Gerald Ford granted amnesty to deserters and "draft dodgers" on the condition that they swear allegiance to the United States and engage in two years of community service. In 1798, President John Adams signed the Alien and Sedition Acts, a set of four laws that restricted criticism of the federal government.

16. When put in the correct order, the paragraph would begin with the following words. 16.____
   A. "Some U.S. government..."
   B. "In May 1865, when..."
   C. "A century later, the..."
   D. "In 1798, President..."

17. If put in logical order, what sentence number would the sentence that begins "President Abraham Lincoln..." be? 17.____
   A. One
   B. Six
   C. Five
   D. Two

18. The author wants to split this paragraph into three separate paragraphs. The THIRD paragraph should begin with the words 18.____
   A. "The issue of amnesty again..."
   B. "In 1798, President..."
   C. "In 1977, President Jimmy..."
   D. "A century later, the..."

19. When organized in sequential order, the last sentence of the paragraph would end with the words 19.____
   A. "...of his political rivals."
   B. "...after the devastating war."
   C. "...them unconditional amnesty."
   D. "...of the federal government."

Questions 20-22.

DIRECTIONS: Questions 20 through 22 are to be answered on the basis of the following passage.

Throughout history, militias have played an important role in national defense against foreign invaders or oppressors. In the original American colonies, state militias served to keep order and played an important role in the fight for independence from the British during the American Revolutionary War. Since that time, state-level militias have continued to exist in the United States alongside a national standing army, providing additional reserve defense and emergency assistance when needed. Some countries still rely almost entirely on public militias for civil defense. In Switzerland, for example, all able-bodied males must serve as part of the Swiss military or civilian service for several months starting when they turn 20 years old and remain reserve militia for years after. Similarly, in Israel, all non-Arab citizens over the age of 18 are required to serve in the Israel Defense Forces for at least two years; Israel is unique in that it requires military service from female citizens as well as males.

20. When put into the correct order, the paragraph should begin with the words 20.____
    A. "Throughout history, militias..." B. "Similarly, in Israel..."
    C. "Some countries still rely..." D. "Since that time, state-level..."

21. The fifth sentence of the paragraph should end with the words 21.____
    A. "...against foreign invaders or oppressors."
    B. "...militias for civil defense."
    C. "...reserve militia for years after."
    D. "...citizens as well as males."

22. The last sentence of the paragraph should end with the words 22.____
    A. "...militias for civil defense."
    B. "...citizens as well as males."
    C. "...against foreign invaders or oppressors."
    D. "...during the American Revolutionary War."

Questions 23-25.

DIRECTIONS: Questions 23 through 25 are to be answered on the basis of the following passage.

Medicines such as herbal and homeopathic remedies differ radically from those typically prescribed by mainstream physicians. These practices derive from different cultural traditions and scientific premises. As of 2012, the Memorial Sloan-Kettering Cancer Center offered hypnosis and tai chi, which is an ancient Chinese exercise, to help eases the pains associated with conventional cancer treatments. Some medical professionals staunchly dismiss a number of alternative techniques and theories as quackery. The concept of alternative medicine encompasses an extremely wide range of therapeutic modalities, from acupuncture to yoga. As of 2012, nearly 40 percent of Americans use some alternative medicines or therapies, according to the National Institutes of Health's National Center for Complementary and Alternative Medicine. Alternative approaches to health, fitness, disease prevention, and treatment are sometimes referred to as holistic health care or natural medicine. These names suggest some of the philosophical foundations shared by traditions such as homeopathy, naturopathy, traditional Chinese medicine and herbal medicine. A University of Pennsylvania study in 2010 found that more than 70 percent of U.S. cancer centers offered information on complementary therapies. Increasingly, health care providers are encouraging patients to combine alternative and conventional (or allopathic) treatments, a practice known as complementary or integrative medicine. In the contemporary United States, the phrase alternative medicine has come to mean virtually any healing or wellness practice not based within the conventional system of medical doctors, nurses, and hospitals. Some of these alternative treatments include acupuncture to alleviate pain and nausea and yoga to help reduce stress and manage pain. Yet taken as a whole, the alternative sector of the health field is enormously popular and rapidly growing. The Health Services Research Journal reported in 2011 that three out of four U.S. health care workers used complementary or alternative medicine practices themselves. Other studies have shown that more medical professionals are recommending that cancer patients seek alternative treatments to deal with the side effects of conventional treatments, such as chemotherapy, radiation, and surgery.

23. When put in the correct order, the first sentence should begin with the words 23.____
    A. "A University of Pennsylvania study..."
    B. "Other studies have shown that..."
    C. "Increasingly, health care providers..."
    D. "In the contemporary United States..."

24. If the author were to split the paragraph into two separate ones, the first sentence of the second paragraph should begin with the words 24.____
    A. "Alternative approaches to health..."
    B. "The concept of alternative medicine..."
    C. "As of 2012, nearly 40%..."
    D. "These names suggest some..."

25. When put into the correct logical sequence, the paragraph should end with the words 25.____
    A. "...Complementary and Alternative Medicine."
    B. "...system of medical doctors, nurses, and hospitals."
    C. "...associated with conventional cancer treatments."
    D. "...health care or natural medicine."

KEY (CORRECT ANSWERS)

1.	A	11.	C
2.	C	12.	B
3.	B	13.	C
4.	D	14.	B
5.	B	15.	A
6.	C	16.	D
7.	D	17.	B
8.	A	18.	D
9.	A	19.	C
10.	D	20.	A

21.	C
22.	B
23.	D
24.	A
25.	C

PREPARING WRITTEN MATERIAL

EXAMINATION SECTION

TEST 1

DIRECTIONS: Each of the sentences in this test may be classified under one of the following four categories:

A. Faulty because of incorrect grammar or word usage
B. Faulty because of incorrect punctuation
C. Faulty because of incorrect capitalization or incorrect spelling
D. Correct

Examine each sentence carefully to determine under which of the above four options it is best classified. Then, in the space to the right, print the capital letter preceding the option which is the BEST of the four suggested above. (Note that each faulty sentence contains but one type of error. Consider a sentence to be correct if it contains none of the types of errors mentioned, even though there may be other correct ways of expressing the same thought.)

1. He sent the notice to the clerk who you hired yesterday. 1.____

2. It must be admitted, however that you were not informed of this change. 2.____

3. Only the employee who have served in this grade for at least two years are eligible for promotion. 3.____

4. The work was divided equally between she and Mary. 4.____

5. He thought that you were not available at that time. 5.____

6. When the messenger returns; please give him this package. 6.____

7. The new secretary prepared, typed, addressed, and delivered, the notices. 7.____

8. Walking into the room, his desk can be seen at the rear. 8.____

9. Although John has worked here longer than She, he produces a smaller amount of work. 9.____

10. She said she could of typed this report yesterday. 10.____

11. Neither one of these procedures are adequate for the efficient performance of this task. 11.____

12. The typewriter is the tool of the typist; the cash register, the tool of the cashier. 12.____

13. "The assignment must be completed as soon as possible" said the supervisor. 13.____

14. As you know, office handbooks are issued to all new Employees. 14.____

15. Writing a speech is sometimes easier than to deliver it before an audience. 15.____

16. Mr. Brown our accountant, will audit the accounts next week. 16.____

17. Give the assignment to whomever is able to do it most efficiently. 17.____

18. The supervisor expected either your or I to file these reports. 18.____

KEY (CORRECT ANSWERS)

1.	A	11.	A
2.	B	12.	C
3.	D	13.	B
4.	A	14.	C
5.	D	15.	A
6.	B	16.	B
7.	B	17.	A
8.	A	18.	A
9.	C		
10.	A		

TEST 2

DIRECTIONS: Each of the sentences in this test may be classified under one of the following four categories:

A. Faulty because of incorrect grammar or word usage
B. Faulty because of incorrect punctuation
C. Faulty because of incorrect capitalization or incorrect spelling
D. Correct

Examine each sentence carefully to determine under which of the above four options it is best classified. Then, in the space to the right, print the capital letter preceding the option which is the BEST of the four suggested above. (Note that each faulty sentence contains but one type of error. Consider a sentence to be correct if it contains none of the types of errors mentioned, even though there may be other correct ways of expressing the same thought.)

1. The fire apparently started in the storeroom, which is usually locked. 1.____

2. On approaching the victim, two bruises were noticed by this officer. 2.____

3. The officer, who was there examined the report with great care. 3.____

4. Each employee in the office had a seperate desk. 4.____

5. All employees including members of the clerical staff, were invited to the lecture. 5.____

6. The suggested Procedure is similar to the one now in use. 6.____

7. No one was more pleased with the new procedure than the chauffeur. 7.____

8. He tried to persaude her to change the procedure. 8.____

9. The total of the expenses charged to petty cash were high. 9.____

10. An understanding between him and I was finally reached. 10.____

KEY (CORRECT ANSWERS)

1.	D	6.	C
2.	A	7.	D
3.	B	8.	C
4.	C	9.	A
5.	B	10.	A

TEST 3

DIRECTIONS: Each of the sentences in this test may be classified under one of the following four categories:

A. Faulty because of incorrect grammar or word usage
B. Faulty because of incorrect punctuation
C. Faulty because of incorrect capitalization or incorrect spelling
D. Correct

Examine each sentence carefully to determine under which of the above four options it is best classified. Then, in the space to the right, print the capital letter preceding the option which is the BEST of the four suggested above. (Note that each faulty sentence contains but one type of error. Consider a sentence to be correct if it contains none of the types of errors mentioned, even though there may be other correct ways of expressing the same thought.)

1. They told both he and I that the prisoner had escaped. 1.____

2. Any superior officer, who, disregards the just complaint of his subordinates, is remiss in the performance of his duty. 2.____

3. Only those members of the national organization who resided in the Middle West attended the conference in Chicago. 3.____

4. We told him to give the national organization assignment to whoever was available. 4.____

5. Please do not disappoint and embarass us by not appearing in court. 5.___

6. Although the office's speech proved to be entertaining, the topic was not relevent to the main theme of the conference. 6.____

7. In February all new officers attended a training course in which they were learned in their principal duties and the fundamental operating procedure of the department. 7.____

8. I personally seen inmate Jones threaten inmates Smith and Green with bodily harm if they refused to participate in the plot. 8.____

9. To the layman, who on a chance visit to the prison observes everything functioning smoothly, the maintenance of prison discipline may seem to be a relatively easily realizable objective. 9.____

10. The prisoners in cell block fourty were forbidden to sit on the cell cots during the recreation hour. 10.____

KEY (CORRECT ANSWERS)

1.	A	6.	C
2.	B	7.	A
3.	C	8.	A
4.	D	9.	D
5.	C	10.	C

TEST 4

DIRECTIONS: Each of the sentences in this test may be classified under one of the following four categories:

A. Faulty because of incorrect grammar or word usage
B. Faulty because of incorrect punctuation
C. Faulty because of incorrect capitalization or incorrect spelling
D. Correct

Examine each sentence carefully to determine under which of the above four options it is best classified. Then, in the space to the right, print the capital letter preceding the option which is the BEST of the four suggested above. (Note that each faulty sentence contains but one type of error. Consider a sentence to be correct if it contains none of the types of errors mentioned, even though there may be other correct ways of expressing the same thought.)

1. I cannot encourage you any. 1.____

2. You always look well in those sort of clothes. 2.____

3. Shall we go to the park? 3.____

4. The man whome he introduced was Mr. Carey. 4.____

5. She saw the letter laying here this morning. 5.____

6. It should rain before the Afternoon is over. 6.____

7. They have already went home. 7.____

8. That Jackson will be elected is evident. 8.____

9. He does not hardly approve of us. 9.____

10. It was he, who won the prize. 10.____

KEY (CORRECT ANSWERS)

1.	A	6.	C
2.	A	7.	A
3.	D	8.	D
4.	C	9.	A
5.	A	10.	B

TEST 5

DIRECTIONS: Each of the sentences in this test may be classified under one of the following four categories:

A. Faulty because of incorrect grammar or word usage
B. Faulty because of incorrect punctuation
C. Faulty because of incorrect capitalization or incorrect spelling
D. Correct

Examine each sentence carefully to determine under which of the above four options it is best classified. Then, in the space to the right, print the capital letter preceding the option which is the BEST of the four suggested above. (Note that each faulty sentence contains but one type of error. Consider a sentence to be correct if it contains none of the types of errors mentioned, even though there may be other correct ways of expressing the same thought.)

1. Shall we go to the park. 1.____

2. They are, alike, in this particular way. 2.____

3. They gave the poor man sume food when he knocked on the door. 3.____

4. I regret the loss caused by the error. 4.____

5. The students' will have a new teacher. 5.____

6. They sweared to bring out all the facts. 6.____

7. He decided to open a branch store on 33rd street. 7.____

8. His speed is equal and more than that of a racehorse. 8.____

9. He felt very warm on that Summer day. 9.____

10. He was assisted by his friend, who lives in the next house. 10.____

KEY (CORRECT ANSWERS)

1.	B	6.	A
2.	B	7.	C
3.	C	8.	A
4.	D	9.	C
5.	B	10.	D

TEST 6

DIRECTIONS: Each of the sentences in this test may be classified under one of the following four categories:

A. Faulty because of incorrect grammar or word usage
B. Faulty because of incorrect punctuation
C. Faulty because of incorrect capitalization or incorrect spelling
D. Correct

Examine each sentence carefully to determine under which of the above four options it is best classified. Then, in the space to the right, print the capital letter preceding the option which is the BEST of the four suggested above. (Note that each faulty sentence contains but one type of error. Consider a sentence to be correct if it contains none of the types of errors mentioned, even though there may be other correct ways of expressing the same thought.)

1. The climate of New York is colder than California. 1.____

2. I shall wait for you on the corner. 2.____

3. Did we see the boy who, we think, is the leader. 3.____

4. Being a modest person, John seldom talks about his invention. 4.____

5. The gang is called the smith street bos. 5.____

6. He seen the man break into the store. 6.____

7. We expected to lay still there for quite a while. 7.____

8. He is considered to be the Leader of his organization. 8.____

9. Although I recieved an invitation, I won't go. 9.____

10. The letter must be here some place. 10.____

KEY (CORRECT ANSWERS)

1.	A	6.	A
2.	D	7.	A
3.	B	8.	C
4.	D	9.	C
5.	C	10.	A

TEST 7

DIRECTIONS: Each of the sentences in this test may be classified under one of the following four categories:

A. Faulty because of incorrect grammar or word usage
B. Faulty because of incorrect punctuation
C. Faulty because of incorrect capitalization or incorrect spelling
D. Correct

Examine each sentence carefully to determine under which of the above four options it is best classified. Then, in the space to the right, print the capital letter preceding the option which is the BEST of the four suggested above. (Note that each faulty sentence contains but one type of error. Consider a sentence to be correct if it contains none of the types of errors mentioned, even though there may be other correct ways of expressing the same thought.)

1. I though it to be he. 1.____

2. We expect to remain here for a long time. 2.____

3. The committee was agreed. 3.____

4. Two-thirds of the building are finished. 4.____

5. The water was froze. 5.____

6. Everyone of the salesmen must supply their own car. 6.____

7. Who is the author of Gone With the Wind? 7.____

8. He marched on and declaring that he would never surrender. 8.____

9. Who shall I say called? 9.____

10. Everyone has left but they. 10.____

KEY (CORRECT ANSWERS)

1.	A	6.	A
2.	D	7.	B
3.	D	8.	A
4.	A	9.	D
5.	A	10.	D

TEST 8

DIRECTIONS: Each of the sentences in this test may be classified under one of the following four categories:

A. Faulty because of incorrect grammar or word usage
B. Faulty because of incorrect punctuation
C. Faulty because of incorrect capitalization or incorrect spelling
D. Correct

Examine each sentence carefully to determine under which of the above four options it is best classified. Then, in the space to the right, print the capital letter preceding the option which is the BEST of the four suggested above. (Note that each faulty sentence contains but one type of error. Consider a sentence to be correct if it contains none of the types of errors mentioned, even though there may be other correct ways of expressing the same thought.)

1. Who did we give the order to? 1.____

2. Send your order in immediately. 2.____

3. I believe I paid the Bill. 3.____

4. I have not met but one person. 4.____

5. Why aren't Tom, and Fred, going to the dance? 5.____

6. What reason is there for him not going? 6.____

7. The seige of Malta was a tremendous event. 7.____

8. I was there yesterday I assure you 8.____

9. Your ukulele is better than mine. 9.____

10. No one was there only Mary. 10.____

KEY (CORRECT ANSWERS)

1.	A	6.	A
2.	D	7.	C
3.	C	8.	B
4.	A	9.	C
5.	B	10.	A

TEST 9

DIRECTIONS: In each of the following groups of sentences, one of the four sentences is faulty in grammar, punctuation, or capitalization. Select the INCORRECT sentence in each case.

1. A. If you had stood at home and done your homework, you would not have failed in arithmetic. 1.____
   B. Her affected manner annoyed every member of the audience.
   C. How will the new law affect our income taxes?
   D. The plants were not affected by the long, cold winter, but they succumbed to the drought of summer.

2. A. He is one of the most able men who have been in the Senate. 2.____
   B. It is he who is to blame for the lamentable mistake.
   C. Haven't you a helpful suggestion to make at this time?
   D. The money was robbed from the blind man's cup.

3. A. The amount of children in this school is steadily increasing. 3.____
   B. After taking an apple from the table, she went out to play.
   C. He borrowed a dollar from me.
   D. I had hoped my brother would arrive before me.

4. A. Whom do you think I hear from every week? 4.____
   B. Who do you think is the right man for the job?
   C. Who do you think I found in the room?
   D. He is the man whom we considered a good candidate for the presidency.

5. A. Quietly the puppy laid down before the fireplace. 5.____
   B. You have made your bed; now lie in it.
   C. I was badly sunburned because I had lain too long in the sun.
   D. I laid the doll on the bed and left the room.

KEY (CORRECT ANSWERS)

1. A
2. D
3. A
4. C
5. A

GLOSSARY OF PERSONNEL TERMS

CONTENTS

GLOSSARY OF PERSONNEL TERMS

A

Abandonment of Position—When an employee quits work without resigning. (715)

Absence Without Leave (AWOL) Absence — without prior approval, therefore without pay, that may be subject to disciplinary action. See also, *Leave Without Pay,* which is an approved absence. (630)

Administrative Workweek— A period of seven consecutive calendar days designated in advance by the head of the agency. Usually an administrative workweek coincides with a calendar week. (610)

Admonishment— Informal reproval of an employee by a supervisor; usually oral, but some agencies require written notice. (751)

Adverse Action— A removal, suspension, furlough without pay for 30 days or less, or reduction-in-grade or pay. An adverse action may be taken against an employee for disciplinary or non-disciplinary reasons. However, if the employee is covered by FPM part 752, the action must be in accordance with those procedures. Removals or reductions-in-grade based solely on unacceptable performance are covered by Part 432. Actions taken for reductions-in-force reasons are covered by Part 351. (752)

Affirmative Action — A policy followed closely by the Federal civil service that requires agencies to take positive steps to insure equal opportunity in employment, development, advancement, and treatment of all employees and applicants for employment regardless of race, color, sex, religion, national origin, or physical or mental handicap. Affirmative action also requires that specific actions be directed at the special problems and unique concerns in assuring equal employment opportunity for minorities, women and other disadvantaged groups.

Agreement—See *Collective Bargaining.*

Annuitant—A retired Federal civil service employee or a survivor (spouse or children) being paid an annuity from the Retirement Fund. (831)

Annuity—Payments to a former employee who retired, or to the surviving spouse or children. It is computed as an annual rate but paid monthly. (831)

Appeal—A request by an employee for review of an agency action by an outside agency: The right to such review-is provided by law or regulation and may include an adversary-type hearing and a written decision in which a finding of facts is made and applicable law, Executive order and regulations are applied.

Appointing Officer—A person having power by law or lawfully delegated authority to make appointments. (210, 311)

Appointment, Noncompetitive— Employment without competing with others, in the sense that it is done without regard to civil service registers, etc. Includes reinstatements, transfers, reassignments, demotions, and promotion. (335)

Appointment, Superior Qualifications—Appointment of a candidate to a position in grade 11 or above of the General Schedule at a rate above the minimum because of the candidate's superior qualifications. A rate above the minimum for the grade must be justified by the applicant's unusually high or unique qualifications, a special need of the Government for the candidate's services, or because the candidate's current pay is higher than the minimum for the grade which he or she is offered. (338, 531)

Appointment, TAPER—Abbreviation for "temporary appointment pending establishment of a register." Employment made under an OPM authority granted to an agency when there are insufficient eligibles on a register appropriate to fill the position involved. (316)

Appointment, Temporary Limited—Nonpermanent appointment of an employee hired for a specified time of one year or less, or for seasonal or intermittent positions. (316)

Appointment, Term—Nonpermanent appointment of an employee hired to work on a project expected to last over one year, but less than four years. (316)

Appropriate Unit —A group of employees which a labor organization seeks to represent for the purpose of negotiating agreements; an aggregation of employees which has a clear and identifiable community of interest and which promotes effective dealings and efficiency of operations. It may be established on a plant or installation, craft, functional or other basis. (Also known as bargaining unit, appropriate bargaining unit.) (711)

Arbitration—Final step of the negotiated grievance procedure which may be invoked by the agency or the union (not the employee) if the grievance has not been resolved. Involves use of an impartial arbitrator selected by the agency and union to render a binding award to resolve the grievance. (711)

Arbitrator—An impartial third party to whom disputing parties submit their differences for decision (award). An *ad hoc* arbitrator is one selected to act in a specific case or a limited group of cases. A permanent arbitrator is one selected to serve for the life of the agreement or a stipulated term, hearing all disputes that arise during this period. (711)

Area Office (OPM)—Forcal point for administering and implementing all OPM programs, except investigations, in the geographic area assigned. Provides personnel management advice and assistance to agencies, and personnel evaluation, recruiting and examining and special program leadership. Principal source of employment information for agencies and the public.

Audit, Work—Visit to an employee or his supervisor to verify or gather information about a position. Sometimes called "desk audit."

B

Bargaining Rights—Legally recognized right of the labor organization to represent employees in negotiations with employers. (711)

Bargaining Unit—An appropriate grouping of employees represented on an exclusive basis by a labor organization. "Appropriate" for this purpose means that it is a grouping of employees who share a community of interest and which promotes effective union and agency dealings and efficient agency operations. (711)

Basic Workweek—For a full-time employee, the 40-hour non overtime work schedule within an administrative workweek. The usual workweek consists of five 8-hour days, Monday through Friday. (610)

Break in Service—The time between separation and reemployment that may cause a loss of rights or privileges. For transfer purposes, it means not being on an agency payroll for one working day or more. For the three-year career conditional period or for reinstatement purposes, it means not being on an agency payroll for over 30 calendar days. (315)

Bumping—During reduction-in-force, the displacement of one employee by another employee in a higher group or subgroup. (351)

C

Career—Tenure of a permanent employee in the competitive service who has completed three years of substantially continuous creditable Federal service. (315)

Career-Conditional—Tenure of a permanent employee in the competitive service who *has not* completed three years of substantially continuous creditable Federal service. (315)

Career Counseling—Service available to employees to assist them in: (1) assessing their skills, abilities, interests, and aptitudes; (2) determining qualifications required for occupations within the career system and how the requirements relate to their individual capabilities; (3) defining their career goals and developing plans for reaching the goals; (4) identifying and assessing education and training opportunities and enrollment procedures; (5) identifying factors which may impair career development; and (6) learning about resources, inside or outside the agency, where additional help is available. (250)

Career Development—Systematic development designed to increase an employee's potential for advancement and career change. It may include classroom training, reading, work experience, etc. (410)

Career Ladder—A career ladder is a series of developmental positions of increasing difficulty in the same line of work, through which an employee may progress to a journeyman level on his or her personal development and performance in that series.

Career Reserved Position—A position within SES that has a specific requirement for impartiality. May be filled" only by career appointment. (920)

Ceiling, Personnel—The maximum number of employees authorized at a given time. (312)

Certification—The process by which eligibles are ranked, according to regulations, for appointment or promotion consideration. (332, 335)

Certification, Selective—Certifying only the names of eligibles who have special qualifications required to fill particular vacant positions. (332)

Certification, Top of the Register—Certifying in regular order, beginning with the eligibles at the top of the register. (332)

Change in Duty Station—A personnel action that changes an employee from one geographical location to another in the same agency. (296)

Change to Lower Grade—Downgrading a position or reducing an employee's grade. See *Demotion.* (296)

Class of Positions—All positions sufficiently similar in: (1) kind or subject matter of work; (2) level of difficulty and responsibility; and (3) qualification requirements, so as to warrant similar treatment in personnel and pay administration. For example, all Grade GS-3 Clerk-Typist positions. (511)

Classified Service—See *Competitive Service* (212)

Collective Bargaining—Performance of the mutual obligation of the employer and the exclusive (employee) representative to meet at reasonable times, to confer and negotiate in good faith, and to execute a written agreement with respect to conditions of employment, except that by any such obligation neither party shall be compelled to agree to proposals, or be required to make concessions. (Also known as collective negotiations, negotiations, and negotiation of agreement.) (711)

Collective Bargaining Agreement—A written agreement between management and a labor-organization which is usually for a definite term, and usually defines conditions of employment, and includes grievance and arbitration procedures. The terms "collective bargaining agreement" and "contract" are synonymous. (711)

Collective Bargaining Unit—A group of employees recognized as appropriate for representation by a labor organization for collective bargaining. (See *Appropriate Unit)* (711)

Compensatory Time Off—Time off (hour-for-hour) granted an employee in lieu of overtime pay. (550)

Competitive Area—For reduction-in-force, that part of an agency within which employees are in competition for retention. Generally, it is that part of an agency covered by a single appointing office. (351)

Competitive Service—Federal positions normally filled through open competitive examination (hence the term "competitive service") under civil service rules and regulations. About 86 percent of all Federal positions are in the competitive service. (212)

Competitive Status—Basic eligibility of a person to be selected to fill a position in the competitive service without open competitive examination. Competitive status may be acquired by career-conditional or career appointment through open competitive examination, or may be granted by statute, executive order, or civil service rules without competitive examination. A person with competitive status may be promoted, transferred, reassigned, reinstated, or demoted subject to the conditions prescribed by civil service rules and regulations. (212)

Consultant—An advisor to an officer or instrumentality of the Government, as distinguished from an officer or employee who carries out the agency's duties and responsibilities. (304)

Consultation—The obligation of an agency to consult the labor organization on particular personnel issues. The process of consultation lies between notification to the labor organization, which may amount simply to providing information, and negotiation, which implies agreement on the part of the labor organization. (711)

Conversion—The process of changing a person's tenure from one type of appointment to another (e.g., conversion from temporary to career-conditional). (315)

D

Demotion—A change of an employee, while serving continuously with the same agency:
(a) To a lower grade when both the old and the new positions are in the General Schedule or under the same type graded wage schedule; or
(b) To a position with a lower rate of pay when both the old and the new positions are under the same type ungraded wage schedule, or are in different pay method categories. (335, 752)

Detail—A temporary assignment of an employee to different duties or to a different position for a specified time, with the employee returning to his/her regular duties at the end of the detail. (300)

Differentials—Recruiting incentives in the form of compensation adjustments justified by: (1) extraordinarily difficult living conditions; (2) excessive physical hardship; or (3) notably unhealthful conditions. (591)

Disciplinary Action—Action taken to correct the conduct of an employee; may range from an admonishment through reprimand, suspension, reduction in grade or pay, to removal from the service. (751, 752)

Displaced Employee Program—(DEP)— A system to help find jobs for career and career-conditional employees displaced either through reduction-in-force or by an inability to accept assignment to another commuting area. (330)

Downgrading—Change of a position to a lower grade. (511, 532)

Dual Compensation—When an employee receives compensation for more than one Federal position if he/she worked more than 40 hours during the week. The term is also used in connection with compensation from a full-time Federal position as well as a retirement annuity for prior military service. (550)

Duty Station—The specific geographical area in which an employee is permanently assigned. (296)

E

Eligible—Any applicant for appointment or promotion who meets the minimum qualification requirements. (337)

Employee Development—A term which may include *career development* and *upward mobility.* It may be oriented toward development for better performance on an employee's current job, for learning a new policy or procedure, or for enhancing an employee's potential for advancement. (410, 412)

Employee, Exempt—An employee exempt from the overtime provisions of the Fair Labor Standards Act. (551)

Employee, Nonexempt—An employee subject to the overtime provision of the Fair Labor Standards Act. (551)

Employee Organization— See *Labor Organization.*

Employee Relations—The personnel function which centers upon the relationship between the supervisor and individual employees. (711)

Entrance Level Position—A position in an occupation at the beginning level grade. (511)

Environmental Differential—Additional pay authorized for a duty involving unusually severe hazards or working conditions. (532, 550)

Equal Employment Opportunity—Federal policy to provide equal employment opportunity for all; to prohibit discrimination on the grounds of age, race, color, religion, sex, national origin, or physical or mental handicap; and to promote the full realization of employees' potential through a continuing affirmative action program in each executive department and agency. (713)

Equal Employment Opportunity Commission—Regulates and enforces the Federal program for insuring equal employment opportunity, and oversees the development and implementation of Federal agencies' affirmative action programs.

Equal Pay for Substantially Equal Work—An underlying principle that provides the same pay level for work at the same level of difficulty and responsibility. (271)
Examination, Assembled—An examination which includes as one of its parts a written or performance test for which applicants are required to assemble at appointed times and places. (337)

Examination— A means of measuring, in a practical and suitable manner, qualifications of applicants for employment in specific positions. (337)

Examination, Fitness-For-Duty—An agency directed examination given by a Federal medical officer or an employee-designated, agency-approved physician to determine the employee's physical, mental, or emotional ability to perform assigned duties safely and efficiently. (339, 831)

Examination, Unassembled—An examination in which applicants are rated on their education, experience, and other qualifications as shown in the formal application and any supportive evidence that may be required, without assembling for a written or performance test. (337)

Excepted Service—Positions in the Federal civil service not subject to the appointment requirements of the competitive service. Exceptions to the normal, competitive requirements are authorized by law, executive order, or regulation. (213, 302)

Exclusive Recognition—The status conferred on a labor organization which receives a majority of votes cast in a representation election, entitling it to act for and negotiate agreements covering all employees included in an appropriate bargaining unit. The labor organization enjoying this status is known as the exclusive representative, exclusive bargaining representative, bargaining agent, or exclusive bargaining agent. (711)

Executive Inventory—An OPM computerized file which contains background information on all members of the Senior Executive Service and persons in positions at GS-16 through GS-18 or the equivalent, and individuals at lower grades who have been certified as meeting the managerial criteria for SES. It is used as an aid to agencies in executive recruiting and as a planning and management tool. (920)

Executive Resources Board—Panel of top agency executives responsible under the law for conducting the merit staffing process for career appointment to Senior Executive Service (SES) positions in the agency. Most Boards are also responsible for setting policy on and overseeing such areas as SES position planning and executive development. (920)

F

Federal Labor Relations Authority (FLRA)—Administers the Federal service labor-management relations program. It resolves questions of union representation of employees; prosecutes and adjudicates allegations of unfair labor practices; decides questions of what is or is not negotiable; and on appeal, reviews decisions of arbitrators. (5 USC 7104)

Federal Personnel Manual (FPM)—The official publication containing Federal personnel regulations and guidance. Also contains the code of Federal civil service law, selected Executive orders pertaining to Federal employment, and civil service rules. (171)

Federal Service Impasses Panel (FSIP)—Administrative body created to resolve bargaining impasses in the Federal service. The Panel may recommend procedures, including arbitration, for settling impasses, or may settle the impasse itself. Considered the legal alternative to strike in the Federal sector. (711)

Federal Wage System (FWS)—A body of laws and regulations governing the administrative processes related to trades and laboring occupations in the Federal service. (532)

Full Field Investigation—Personal investigation of an applicant's background to determine whether he/she meets fitness standards for a critical-sensitive Federal position. (736)

Function—All, or a clearly identifiable segment, of an agency's mission, including all the parts of the mission (e.g. procurement), regardless of how performed. (351)

G

General Position—A position within the Senior Executive Service that may be filled by a career, noncareer, or limited appointment. (920)

General Schedule—(GS)The graded pay system as presented by Chapter 51 of Title 5, United States Code, for classifying positions. **(511)**

Grade—All classes of positions which, although different with respect to kind or subject matter of work, are sufficiently equivalent as to (1) level of difficulty and responsibility, and (2) level of qualification requirements of the work to warrant the inclusion of such classes of positions within one range of rates of basic compensation. (511, 532)

Grade Retention—The right of a General Schedule or prevailing rate employee, when demoted for certain reasons, to retain the higher grade for most purposes for two years. (536)

Grievance, (Negotiated Procedure)—Any complaint or expressed dissatisfaction by an employee against an action by management in connection with his job, pay or other aspects of employment. Whether such complaint or expressed dissatisfaction is formally recognized and handled as a "grievance" under a negotiated procedure depends on the scope of that procedure. (711)

Grievance (Under Agency Administrative Procedure)—A request by an employee or by a group of employees acting as individuals, for personal relief in a matter of concern or dissatisfaction to the employee, subject to the control of agency management.

Grievance Procedure—A procedure, either administrative or negotiated, by which employees may seek redress of any matter subject to the control of agency management. (711, 771)

H

Handbook X-118— The official qualification standard a manual for General Schedule Positions. (338)

Handbook X-118C—The official qualification standards manual for Wage System positions. (338)

Hearing—The opportunity for contending parties under a grievance, complaint, or other remedial process, to introduce testimony and evidence and to confront and examine or cross examine witnesses. (713, 771, 772)

I

Impasse Procedures—Procedures for resolving deadlocks between agencies and union in collective bargaining. (711)

Incentive Awards—An all-inclusive term covering awards granted under Part 451 or OPM regulations. Includes an award for a suggestion submitted by an employee and adopted by management; a special achievement award for performance exceeding job requirements, or an honorary award in the form of a certificate, emblem, pin or other item. (451)

Indefinite—Tenure of a nonpermanent employee hired for an unlimited time. (316)

Injury, Work Related—For compensation under the Federal Employees' Compensation Act, a personal injury sustained while in the performance of duty. The term "injury" includes diseases proximately caused by the employment. (810)

Injury, Traumatic—Under the Federal Employees' Compensation Act, for continuation of pay purposes, a wound or other condition of the body caused by external force, including stress or strain. The injury must be identifiable by time and place of occurrence and member or function of the body affected, and be caused by a specific event or incident or series of events or incidents within a single day or work shift. (810)

Intergovernmental Personnel Assignment—Assignments of personnel to and from the Executive Branch of the Federal Government, state and local government agencies, and institutions of higher education up to two years, although a two-year extension may be permitted. The purpose is to provide technical assistance or expertise where needed for short periods of time. (334)

Intermittent—Less than full-time employment requiring irregular work hours which cannot be prescheduled. (610)

J

Job Analysis—Technical review and evaluation of a position's duties, responsibilities, and level of work and of the skills, abilities, and knowledge needed to do the work. (511, 532)

Job Enrichment—Carefully planned work assignments and/or training to use and upgrade employee skills, abilities, and interests; and to provide opportunity for growth, and encourage self-improvement. (312)

Job Freeze—A restriction on hiring and/or promotion by administrative or legislative action. (330)

Job Title— The formal name of a position as determined by official classification standards. (511, 532)

Journeyman Level—(Full Performance Level)The lowest level of a career ladder position at which an employee has learned the full range of duties in a specific occupation. All jobs below full performance level are developmental levels, through which each employee in the occupation may progress to full performance. (511)

L

Labor-Management Relations—Relationships and dealings between employee unions and management. (711)

Labor Organization—An organization composed in whole or in part of employees, in which employees participate and pay dues, and which has as a purpose dealing with an agency concerning grievances and working conditions of employment. (711)

Lead Agency—Under the Federal Wage-System, the Federal agency with the largest number of Federal wage workers in a geographical area; consequently, it has the primary role for determining wage rates for all Federal employees who work in that area and are covered by the System. (532)

Leave, Annual—Time allowed to employees for vacation and other absences for personal reasons. (630)

Leave, Court—Time allowed to employees for jury and certain types of witness service. (630)

Leave, Military—Time allowed to employees for certain types of military service. (630)

Leave, Sick—Time allowed to employees for physical incapacity, to prevent the spread of contagious diseases, or to obtain medical, dental or eye examination or treatment. (630)

Leave Without Pay (LWOP)—A temporary nonpay status and absence from duty, requested by an employee. The permissive nature of "leave without pay" distinguishes it from "absence without leave." (630)

Level of Difficulty—A classification term used to indicate the relative ranking of duties and responsibilities. (511, 532)

M

Maintenance Review—A formal, periodic review (usually annual) of all positions in an organization, or portion of an organization, to insure that classifications are correct and position descriptions are current. (511)

Major Duty—Any duty or responsibility, or group of closely related tasks, of a position which (1) determines qualification requirements for the position, (2) occupies a significant amount of the employee's time, and (3) is a regular or recurring duty. (511)

Management Official—An individual employed by an agency in a position whose duties and responsibilities require or authorize the individual to formulate, determine or influence the policies of the agency. (711)

Management Rights—The right of management to make day-today personnel decisions and to direct the work force without mandatory negotiation with the exclusive representative. (See "Reserved Rights Doctrine.") Usually a specific list of management authorities not subject to the obligation to bargain. (117)

Mediation—Procedure using a third-party to facilitate the reaching of an agreement voluntarily. (711)

Merit Promotion Program—The system under which agencies consider an employee for internal personnel actions on the basis of personal merit. (335)

Merit Systems Protection Board (MSPB)—An independent agency which monitors the administration of the Federal civil service system, prosecutes and adjudicates allegations of merit principle abuses, and hears and decides other civil service appeals. (5 USC 1205)

N

National Agency Check and Inquiry (NACI)—The Investigation of applicants for nonsensitive Federal positions by means of a name check through national investigative files and voucher inquiries. (731)

National Consultation Rights—A relationship established between the headquarters of a Federal agency and the national office of a union under criteria of the Federal Labor Relations Authority. When a union holds national consultation rights, the agency must give the union notice of proposed new substantive personnel policies, and of proposed changes in personnel policies, and an opportunity to comment on such proposals. The union has a right to: (1) suggest changes in personnel policies and have those suggestions carefully considered; (2) consult at reasonable times with appropriate officials about personnel policy matters; and (3) submit its views in writing on personnel policy matters at any time. The agency must provide the union with a written statement (which need not be detailed) of reasons for taking its final action on a policy. (711)

Negotiability—A determination as to whether a matter is within the obligation to bargain. (711)

Negotiated Grievance Procedure—A procedure applicable to members of a bargaining unit for considering grievances. Coverage and scope are negotiated by the parties to the agreement, except that the procedures may not cover certain matters designated in Title VII of the CSRA as excluded from the scope of negotiated grievance procedures. (711)

Negotiations—The bargaining process used to reach a settlement between labor and management over conditions of employment. (711)

Nominating Officer—A subordinate officer of an agency to whom authority has been delegated by the head of the agency to nominate for appointment but not actually appoint employees. (311)

O

Objection—A written statement by an agency of the reasons why it believes an eligible whose name is on a certificate is not qualified for the position to which referred. If the Examining Office sustains the objection, the agency may eliminate the person from consideration. (332)

Occupational Group—Positions of differing kinds but within the same field of work. For example, the GS-500 Accounting and Budget Occupational Group includes: General Accounting Clerical and Administrative Series; Financial Management; Internal Revenue Agent Accounting Technician; Payroll; etc. (511, 532)

Office of Personnel Management (OPM)—Regulates, administers, and evaluates the civil service program according to merit principles. (5 USC 1103)

Office of Workers Compensation Programs (OWCP)—In the Department of Labor, administers statutes that allow compensation to employees and their survivors for work-related injuries and illnesses. Decides and pays claims. (810)

Official Personnel Folder (OPF)—The official repository of employment records and documents affecting personnel actions during an employee's Federal civilian service. (293)

Overtime Work—Under Title 5, U.S. Code, officially ordered or approved work performed in excess of eight hours in a day or 40 hours in a week. Under the Fair Labor Standards Act, work in excess of 40 hours in a week by a nonexempt employee. (550, 551)

P

Pass Over—Elimination from appointment consideration of a veteran preference eligible on a certificate (candidate list), to appoint a lower ranking nonveteran, when the agency submits reasons which OPM finds sufficient. (332)

Pay Retention—The right of a General Schedule or prevailing rate employee (following a grade retention period or at other specified times when the rate of basic pay would otherwise be reduced) to continue to receive the higher rate. Pay is retained indefinitely. (536)

Pay, Severance—Money paid to employees separated by reduction-in-force and not eligible for retirement. The following formula is used, but the amount cannot be more than one year's pay:

Basic Severance Pay— One week's pay for each year of civilian service up to 10 years, and two weeks' pay for each year served over 10 years, plus

Age Adjustment Allowance —10 percent of the basic severance pay for each year over age 40. (550)

Performance Appraisal—The comparison, under a performance appraisal system, of an employee's actual performance against the performance standards previously established for the position. (430)

Personal Action— The process necessary to appoint, separate, reinstate, or make other changes affecting an employee (e.g., change in position assignment, tenure, etc.). (296)

Personnel Management—Management of human resources to accomplish a mission and provide individual job satisfaction. It is the line responsibility of the operating supervisor and the staff responsibility of the personnel office. (250)

Position—A specific job consisting of all the current major duties and responsibilities assigned or delegated by management. (312)

Position Change—A promotion, demotion, or reassignment. (335)

Position Classification—Analyzing and categorizing jobs by occupational group, series, class, and grade according to like duties, responsibilities, and qualification requirements. (511, 532)

Position Classifier—A specialist in job analysis who determines the titles, occupational groups, series, and grades of positions. (312)

Position Description—An official written statement of the major duties, responsibilities and supervisory relationships of a position. (312)

Position Management—The process of designing positions to combine logical and consistent duties and responsibilities into an orderly, efficient, and productive organization to accomplish agency mission. (312)

Position Survey—Agency review of positions to determine whether the positions are still needed and, if so, whether the classification and position description are correct. (312)

Position, "PL 313 Type"—Positions established under Public Law 80-313 of August 1, 1947, or similar authorities. A small group of high level professional and scientific positions generally in the competitive service, but not filled through competitive examinations. Salaries are set between GS-12 and GS-18. (534)

Preference, Compensable Disability ("CP")—Ten-point preference awarded to a veteran separated under honorable conditions from active duty, who receives compensation of 10 percent or more for a service-connected disability. Eligible "CP" veterans are placed at the top of civil service lists of eligibles for positions at GS-9 or higher. (211)

Preference, 30 Percent or More, Disabled ("CPS")—A disabled veteran whose disability is rated at 30 percent or more, entitled to special preference in appointment and during reduction in force.

Preference, Disability ("XP")—Ten-point preference in hiring for a veteran separated under honorable conditions from active duty and who has a service-connected disability or receives compensation, pension, or disability retirement from the VA or a uniformed service. (211)

Preference, Mother ("XP")—Ten-point preference to which the mother of a deceased or disabled military veteran may be entitled. (211)

Preference, Spouse ("XP")—Ten-point preference to which a disabled military veteran's spouse may be entitled. (211)

Preference, Tentative ("TP")— Five-point veteran preference tentatively awarded an eligible who served on active duty during specified periods and was separated from military service under honorable conditions. It must be verified by the appointing officer. (211)

Preference, Veteran—The statutory right to special advantage in appointments or separations; based on a person's discharge under honorable conditions from the armed forces, for a service-connected disability. *Not* applicable to the Senior Executive Service. (211)

Preference, Widow or Widower ("XP")—Ten-point preference to which a military veteran's widow or widower may be entitled. (211)

Premium Pay—Additional pay for overtime, night, Sunday and holiday work. (550)

Prevailing Rate System—A subsystem of the Federal Wage System used to determine the employee's pay in a particular wage area. The determination requires, comparing. the_. rate of pay with the private sector for similar duties and responsibilities. (532)

Probationary Period—A trial period which is a condition of the initial competitive appointment. Provides the final indispensable test of ability, that of actual performance on the job. (315)

Promotion—A change of an employee to a higher grade when both the old and new positions are under the same job classification system and pay schedule, or to a position with higher pay in a different job classification system and pay schedule. (335)

Promotion, Career—Promotion of an employee without current competition when: (1) he/ she had earlier been competitively selected from a register or under competitive promotion procedures for an assignment intended as a matter of record to be preparation for the position being filled; or (2) the position is reconstituted at a higher grade because of additional duties and responsibilities. (335)

Promotion, Competitive—Selection of a current or former Federal civil service employee for a higher grade position, using procedures that compare the candidates on merit. (335)

Promotion Certificate—A list of best qualified candidates to be considered to fill a position under competitive promotion procedures. (335)

Q

Qualifications Review Board—A panel attached to OPM that determines whether a candidate for career appointment in the Senior Executive Service meets the managerial criteria established by law.

Qualification Requirements—Education, experience, and other prerequisites to employment or placement in a position. (338)

Quality Graduate—College graduate who was a superior student and can be hired at a higher grade than the one to which he/she would otherwise be entitled '(338)

Quality Increase—An additional within-grade increase granted to General Schedule employees for high quality performance above that ordinarily found in the type of position concerned (531).

R

Reassignment—The change of an employee, while serving continuously within the same agency, from one position to another, without promotion or demotion. (210)

Recognition—Employer acceptance of a labor organization as authorized to negotiate, usually for all members of a bargaining unit. (711) Also, used to refer to incentive awards granted under provisions of Parts 451 and 541 of OPM Regulations, and Quality Increases granted under Part 531.

Recruitment—Process of attracting a supply of qualified eligibles for employment consideration. (332)

Reduction-in-Force (RIF)—A personnel action that may be required due to lack of work or funds, changes resulting from reorganization, downward reclassification of a position, or the need to make room for an employee with reemployment or restoration rights. Involves separating an employee from his/her present position, but does not necessarily result in separation or downgrading. (351) (See also *Tenure Groups.)*

Reemployment Priority List—Career and career-conditional employees, separated by reduction-in-force, who are identified, in priority order, for reemployment to competitive positions in the agency in the commuting area where the separations occurred. (330)

Reemployment Rights—Right of an employee to return to an agency after detail, transfer, or appointment to: (1) another Executive agency during an emergency; (2) an international organization; or (3) other statutorily covered employment, e.g., the Peace Corps. (352)

Register—A list of eligible applicants compiled in the order of their relative standing for referral to Federal jobs, after competitive civil service examination. (332,210)

Reinstatement— Noncompetitive reemployment in the competitive service based on previous service under a career or career-conditional appointment. (315)

Removal—Separation of an employee for cause or because of continual unacceptable performance. (432, 752)

Representation—Actions and rights of the labor organization to consult and negotiate with management on behalf of the bargaining unit and represent employees in the unit. (711)

Representation Election—Election conducted to determine whether the employees in an appropriate unit (See *Bargaining Unit)* desire a labor organization to act as their exclusive representative. (711)

Reprimand—An official rebuke of an employee. Normally in writing and placed in the temporary side of an employee's OPF-(751)

"Reserved Rights Doctrine"—Specific functions delegated to management by Title VII of CSRA that protect management's ability to perform its necessary functions and duties. (See Management Rights.) Delegates to management specific functions not subject to negotiation except as to procedures and impact. (711)

Resignation—A separation, prior to retirement, in response to an employee's request for the action. It is a voluntary expression of the employee's desire to leave the organization and must not be demanded as an alternative to some other action to be taken or withheld. (715)

Restoration Rights—Employees who enter military service or sustain a compensable job-related injury or disability are entitled to be restored to the same or higher employment status held prior to their absence. (353)

Retention Preference—The relative standing of employees competing in a reduction-inforce. Their standing is determined by veteran's preference, tenure group, length of service, and performance appraisal. (351)

Retention Register—A list of all employees, arranged by competitive level, describing their retention preference during reductions-in-force. (351)

Retirement—Payment of an annuity after separation from a position under the Civil Service Retirement System and based on meeting age and length of service requirements. The types of retirement are:

Deferred - An employee with five years civilian service who separates or transfers to a position not under the Retirement Act, may receive an annuity, does not withdraw from the Retirement Fund. (.83:1)

Disability - An immediate annuity paid to an employee under the retirement system who has completed five years of civilian service and has suffered a mental, emotional, or physical disability not the result of the employee's vicious habits, intemperance, or willful misconduct, (831)

Discontinued Service - An immediate annuity paid to an employee who is involuntarily separated, through no personal fault of the employee, after age 50 and 20 years of service, or at any age with 25 years of service. This annuity is reduced by 1/6 of one percent for each full month under age 55 (two percent per year). (831)

Optional - The minimum combinations of age and service for this kind of immediate annuity are: age 62 with five years of service; age 60 with 20 years of service; age 55 with 30 years of service. (831)

Review, Classification—An official written request for reclassification of a position. Previously called a classification appeal.

S

Schedules A, B, and C—Categories of positions excepted from the competitive service by regulation. (213)

Schedule A—Positions other than confidential or policy determining, for which it is not practical to examine.

Schedule B— Positions other than confidential or policy determining for which it is not practical to hold a competitive examination.

Schedule C—Positions of a confidential or policy determining character.

Senior Executive Service—A separate personnel system for persons who set policy and administer programs at the top levels of the Government (equivalent to GS-16 through Executive Level IV). (920)

Service Computation Date-Leave—The date, either actual or adjusted, from which service credit is accumulated for determining the rate of leave accrual; it may be different from the service computation date, which determines relative standing in a subgroup for reduction-in-force, or service computation date for retirement. (296)

Service Record Card (Standard Form 7)—A brief of the employee's service history. It is kept on file in accordance with agency disposition instructions. (295)

Special Salary Rates—Salary rates higher than regular statutory schedule; established for occupations in which private enterprise pays substantially more than the regular Federal Schedule. (530)

Spoils System—The personnel system characterized by the political appointment and removal of employees without regard to merit. (212)

Staffing—Use of available and projected personnel through recruitment, appointment, reassignment, promotion, reduction-in-force, etc., to provide the work force required to fulfill the agency's mission. (250)

Standard Form—171 ("Personal Qualification Statement") Used in applying for a Federal position through a competitive examination. (295)

Standards of Conduct For Labor Organization—In the Federal sector, a code governing internal democratic practices and fiscal responsibility, and procedures to which a labor organization must adhere to be eligible to receive any recognition. (711)

Steward (Union Steward)—A local union's representative in a plant or department, appointed by the union to carry out union duties, adjust grievances, collect dues and solicit new members. Stewards are employees trained by the union to carry out their duties.

Strike—Temporary stoppage of work by a group of employees to express a grievance, enforce a demand for changes in conditions of employment, obtain recognition, or resolve a dispute with management. *Wildcat strike-* a strike not sanctioned by union and which may violate a collective agreement. *Quickie strike-* a spontaneous or unannounced strike of short duration. *Slowdown-a* deliberate reduction of output without an actual strike in order to force concessions from *an* employer. *Walkout* -same as strike. Strikes are illegal for Federal employees. (711)

Suitability—An applicant's or employee's fitness for Federal employment as indicated by character and conduct. (731)

Supervisor—An individual employed by an agency having authority, in the interest of the agency, to hire, direct, assign, promote, reward, transfer, furlough, lay off, recall, suspend, discipline-or remove employees, to adjust their grievances, or to effectively recommend such action-if the exercise of the authority is not merely routine or clerical in nature but requires the consistent exercise of independent judgment. With respect to any unit which includes firefighters or nurses, the term "supervisor" includes only those individuals who devote a preponderance of their employment time to exercising such authority. (711).

Survey, Classification—An intensive study of all positions in an organization or organizational segment to insure their correct classification.

Suspension—Placing an employee, for disciplinary reasons, in a temporary status without duties and pay. (751, 752)

T

Tenure—The time an employee may reasonably expect to serve under a current appointment. It is governed by the type of appointment, without regard to whether the employee has competitive status. (210)

Tenure Groups—Categories of employees ranked in priority order for retention during reduction in force . Within each group, veterans are ranked above nonveterans. For the competitive service, the tenure groups are, in descending order:

Group I—Employees under career appointments and not serving probation.

Group II—Employees serving probation, career-conditional employees, and career employees in obligated positions.

Group III—Employees with indefinite appointments, status quo employees under any other nonstatus, nontemporary appointment. (351)

For the *excepted service,* they are in descending order:

Group I—Permanent employees, not serving a trial period, whose appointments carry no restriction or condition, such as "indefinite" or "time-limited".

Group II—Employees serving trial periods, those whose tenure is indefinite because they occupy obligated positions, and those whose tenure is equivalent to career-conditional in the competitive service.

Group III—Employees whose tenure is indefinite, but not potentially permanent, and temporary employees who have completed one year of current continuous employment. (351)

Tenure Subgroups—The ranking of veterans above nonveterans in each tenure group, as follows:

Subgroup AD—Veterans with service-connected disability of 30% or more.
Subgroup A— All other veterans
Subgroup B—Nonveterans

Time-in-Grade Restriction—A requirement intended to prevent excessively rapid promotions in the General Schedule. Generally, an employee may not be promoted more than two grades within one year to positions up to GS-5. At GS-5 and above, an employee must serve a minimum of one year in grade, and cannot be promoted more than one grade, or two grades if that is the normal progression. (300)

Tour of Duty—The hours of a day (a daily tour of duty) and the day of an administrative workweek (weekly tour of duty) scheduled in advance and during which an employee is required to work regularly. (610)

Training—Formal instruction or controlled and planned exposure to learning. (410)

Transfer—A change of an employee, without a break in service of one full workday, from a position in one agency to a position in another agency. (315)

Transfer of Function—For reduction-in-force, the transfer of a continuing function from one agency or competitive area to another, or when the competitive area in which work is performed is moved to another commuting area. (315)

U

Unemployment Compensation—Income maintenance payments to former Federal employees who: (1) are unemployed; (2) file a claim at a local employment office for unemployment compensation; and (3) register for work assignment. The program is administered through state and D.C. employment service offices, which determine eligibility and make the payments. (850)

Unfair Labor Practices—Prohibited actions by agency management and labor organizations. (711)

Union—See *Labor Organization.*

Upward Mobility—Systematic career development requiring competitive selection in positions that provide experience and training leading to future assignments in other, more responsible positions.(410)

V

Veteran—A person entitled to preference under 5 USC 2108, including a spouse, widow, widower, or mother entitled to preference under the law. (211)

Voucher—In staffing terms, a formal inquiry to employers, references, professors, and others who presumably know a job applicant well enough to describe job qualifications and personal character. (337)

19

W

Wage Employees—Those employees-in trades, crafts, or labor occupations covered by the Federal Wage System, whose pay is fixed and adjusted periodically in accordance with prevailing rates. (532)

Within-Grade Increase—A salary increase provided in certain Government pay plans based upon time-in-grade and acceptable or satisfactory work performance. Also known as "periodic increase" or "step increase." (531)

NOTE:

Numbers in parentheses after the definitions refer to the appropriate FEDERAL PERSONNEL MANUAL (FPM) Chapter indicated.

www.ingramcontent.com/pod-product-compliance
Lightning Source LLC
Chambersburg PA
CBHW081817300426
44116CB00014B/2395
9781799323440